How GREAT IS OUR *God!*

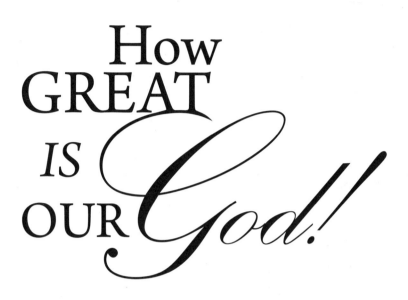

From the Bible-Teaching Ministry of

CHARLES R. SWINDOLL

INSIGHT FOR LIVING

HOW GREAT IS OUR GOD!

From the Bible-Teaching Ministry of Charles R. Swindoll

Charles R. Swindoll has devoted his life to the clear, practical teaching and application of God's Word and His grace. A pastor at heart, Chuck has served as senior pastor to congregations in Texas, Massachusetts, and California. He currently pastors Stonebriar Community Church in Frisco, Texas, but Chuck's listening audience extends far beyond a local church body. As a leading program in Christian broadcasting, *Insight for Living* airs in major Christian radio markets around the world, reaching people groups in languages they can understand. Chuck's extensive writing ministry has also served the body of Christ worldwide and his leadership as president and now chancellor of Dallas Theological Seminary has helped prepare and equip a new generation for ministry. Chuck and Cynthia, his partner in life and ministry, have four grown children and ten grandchildren.

Based upon the original outlines, charts, and transcripts of Charles R. Swindoll's sermons, the Bible Companion text was written by Derrick G. Jeter, Th.M., Dallas Theological Seminary, a writer in the Creative Ministries department of Insight for Living.

Published By:
IFL Publishing House
A Division of Insight for Living
Post Office Box 251007
Plano, Texas 75025-1007

Editor in Chief: Cynthia Swindoll, President, Insight for Living
Executive Vice President: Wayne Stiles, Th.M., D.Min., Dallas Theological Seminary
Theological Editor: John Adair, Th.M., Ph.D., Dallas Theological Seminary
Content Editor: Amy L. Snedaker, B.A., English, Rhodes College
Copy Editors: Jim Craft, M.A., English, Mississippi College
       Melanie Munnell, M.A., Humanities, The University of Texas at Dallas
Project Coordinator, Creative Ministries: Kim Gibbs, Trinity Valley Community College, 1991–1993
Project Coordinator, Communications: Karen Berard, B.A., Mass Communications,
       Texas State University-San Marcos
Proofreader: Paula McCoy, B.A., English, Texas A&M University-Commerce
Cover Design: Margaret Gulliford, B.A., Graphic Design, Taylor University
Production Artist: Nancy Gustine, B.F.A., Advertising Art, University of North Texas
Cover Art: Fotolia.com

ISBN: 978-1-57972-854-0
Printed in the United States of America

Janet Nemec

Table of Contents

A Letter from Chuck

Aiden Wilson Tozer was a man of rare insight and spiritual vision. He is also one of my favorite authors. In a magnificent book he wrote late in life, *The Knowledge of the Holy*, Tozer made an observation that flashes like a gigantic neon stop sign. Every time I read it, I mentally slam on the brakes and screech to a halt.

> It is not a cheerful thought that millions of us who live in a land of Bibles, who belong to churches and labor to promote the Christian religion, may yet pass our whole life on this earth without once having thought or tried to think seriously about the being of God. . . . We prefer to think where it will do more good— about how to build a better mousetrap, for instance, or how to make two blades of grass grow where one grew before. And for this we are now paying a too heavy price in the secularization of our religion and the decay of our inner lives.[1]

Those were strong words in 1961 when Tozer penned them. They remain strong words today—and they are true words. We must face squarely and put into practice what too many of us have long neglected: thinking seriously about our great and triune God— Father, Son, and Holy Spirit.

This book, *How Great Is Our God! Bible Companion*, will help you do just that; it will help you think seriously about God. I suppose we could call this a book of theology, the study of God, but don't let that frighten you. This book wasn't written in an ivory tower by or to an egghead; it was written with you in mind—to reveal the greatness of God in a practical way.

I'm confident that after you've met or rediscovered the Father and His attributes, the Son on the cross, and the Spirit in His power you'll see just how great our God is. When you do, you will declare with Paul, "Oh, the depth of the riches both of the wisdom and knowledge of God! How unsearchable are His judgments and unfathomable His ways!" (Romans 11:33). I'm equally confident that your inner life will bloom with the beauty of love, joy, and peace.

Because wherever God is, there is an abundance of life.

Chuck Swindoll

Charles R. Swindoll

How to Use This Bible Companion

Human beings are curious creatures. We will explore the vastness of outer space and the depths of the oceans to see what we can learn; we'll climb the highest mountains just because they are there and cross scorching deserts to see what is on the other side. We'll even experiment with *avant-garde* religions and new ways of thinking about life. But few of us are curious enough to want to know the truth about the God of the Bible. If you've picked up this book, you must be one of the curious ones. You have a real treat in store, as we set out on a journey to discover the greatness of our God.

In twelve chapters, *How Great Is Our God! Bible Companion* delves into the nature of our triune God. Though the book is not set out in sections, we could divide it into three parts of four chapters each. The first four chapters focus on God the Father, looking at some of His key attributes. The second set of chapters concentrates on Christ, God the Son, and His cross. The last four chapters explore the too often misunderstood person and work of God the Holy Spirit.

You may choose to work through this Bible Companion individually or with a group, but regardless of how you choose to complete this study, a brief introduction to the overall structure of each lesson will help you get the most out of it.

Lesson Organization

 THE HEART OF THE MATTER highlights the main idea of each lesson for rapid orientation. The lesson itself is then composed of two main teaching sections for insight and application:

DISCOVERING THE WAY explores the principles of Scripture through observation and interpretation of the Bible passages, drawing out practical principles for life. Parallel passages and additional questions supplement the main Scriptures for a more in-depth study.

 STARTING YOUR JOURNEY focuses on application, helping you to put into practice the principles of the lesson in ways that fit your personality, gifts, and level of spiritual maturity.

Using the Bible Companion

How Great Is Our God! Bible Companion is designed with individual study in mind, but it may be adapted for group study. If you choose to use this Bible Companion in a group setting, please keep in mind that many of the lessons ask personal, probing questions, seeking to elicit answers that reveal an individual's true character and challenge the reader to change. Therefore, the answers to some of the questions in this Bible Companion may be potentially embarrassing if they are shared in a group setting. Care, therefore, should be taken by the group leader to prepare the group for the sensitive nature of these studies, to forgo certain questions if they appear to be too personal, and to remain perceptive to the mood and dynamics of the group if questions or answers become uncomfortable.

Whether you use this Bible Companion in groups or individually, we recommend the following method:

Prayer — Begin each lesson with prayer, asking God to teach you through His Word and to open your heart to the self-discovery afforded by the questions and text of the lesson.

Scripture — Have your Bible handy. We recommend the New American Standard Bible or another literal translation, rather than a paraphrase. As you progress through each lesson, you'll be prompted to read relevant sections of Scripture and answer questions related to the topic. You will also want to look up the Scripture passages noted in parentheses.

Questions—As you encounter the questions, approach them wisely and creatively. Not every question will be applicable to each person all the time. Use the questions as general guides in your thinking rather than rigid forms to complete. If there are things you just don't understand or that you want to explore further, be sure to jot down your thoughts or questions.

Special Bible Companion Features

Throughout the chapters, you'll find several special features designed to add insight or depth to your study. Use these features to enhance your study and deepen your knowledge of Scripture, history, and theology:

GETTING TO THE ROOT
While our English versions of the Scriptures are reliable, studying the original languages can often bring to light nuances of the text that are sometimes missed in translation. This feature explores the underlying meanings of the words or phrases in a particular passage, sometimes providing parallel examples to illuminate the meaning of the inspired biblical text.

DIGGING DEEPER
Various passages in Scripture touch on deeper theological questions. This feature will help you gain deeper insight into specific theological issues related to the biblical text.

DOORWAY TO HISTORY
Sometimes the chronological gap that separates us from the original author and readers clouds our understanding of a passage of Scripture. This feature takes you back in time to explore the surrounding history, culture, and customs of the ancient world.

Our prayer is that this Insight for Living Bible Companion will not only help you to dig deeper into God's Word but also provide insights and application for *real* life.

How GREAT IS OUR *God!*

Lesson One

The Glory of God
2 Chronicles 26; Isaiah 42:5–8

THE HEART OF THE MATTER

If the whole human race were suddenly struck blind, the sun would continue to shine by day and the moon by night. If humanity were suddenly unable to hear, birds would continue to sing and brooks to babble. If Christians were suddenly overcome by sinful self-conceit—the dull and darkening attempt to steal God's glory—His supremacy would remain undiminished. We learn from the tragic life of King Uzziah that God's glory is His and His alone, and He shares it with no other.

DISCOVERING THE WAY

America's sixth president had a privileged childhood. He was afforded opportunities to study and to travel the world that even learned and wealthy men of his day couldn't fathom. A man of science and letters, he served as Secretary of State before becoming President of the United States. Yet, John Quincy Adams—like John Adams, his famous father—possessed a key character flaw: he was, in the old vernacular, vainglorious.

In a letter to John Quincy from his sharp-tongued mother, Abigail, in regard to his boastful manner, she scolded,

> If you are conscious to yourself that you possess more knowledge upon some subjects than others of your standing, reflect that you have had greater opportunities of seeing the world and obtaining a knowledge of mankind than any of your contemporaries. . . . How

unpardonable would it have been in you to have been a blockhead.[1]

Thousands of years before, in the kingdom of Judah, lived another young man with a similar background and character defect as John Quincy Adams. This young man became a godly king, but he ended his reign as a "blockhead" because he vaingloriously tried to steal God's glory.

How would you define *glory*? How does the dictionary define it?

_____

_____

_____

_____

GETTING TO THE ROOT
Too Heavy a Word to Toss Around Lightly

Before the temple was built in Jerusalem, Israelites worshiped God in a "tabernacle." A portable tent, constructed in the desert while the people made their way to the Promised Land, the tabernacle became a "house" for God whenever they stopped. Exodus 40 describes the first time the tabernacle was erected and God took up "residence" in it. As Moses recorded: "the cloud covered the tent of meeting, and the [blinding] glory of the LORD filled the tabernacle" (Exodus 40:34).

But what does it mean that God's "glory" filled the tabernacle? The Hebrew word for glory is *kabod* and basically means "heavy."[2] When *kabod* is associated with God's visible presence, as in Exodus 40:34–35, it takes on a special meaning—the heaviness of God's holiness. In the words of one Hebrew scholar, "God wishes to dwell with men, to have his reality and his splendor [glory] known to them. But this is only possible when they take account of the stunning quality of his holiness."[3]

Like dew weighing heavy in the air, so God's holy presence, His glory, was heavy in the tabernacle — it permeated everything around it. Christians who carry the presence of God within them, in the person of the indwelling Holy Spirit, do well in not taking lightly God's glory, just as Moses didn't when he couldn't enter the tabernacle because of the heaviness of God (Exodus 40:35).

A Declaration Most Have Forgotten

The glory of God is something we should not take lightly — God doesn't. He guards His glory jealously because it represents His essential reality, as the book of Isaiah reminds us.

 Read Isaiah 42:5–8.

After Isaiah's cleansing encounter in the presence of God, where the reality of God's holiness hung heavy in the air (Isaiah 6:1–8), Isaiah declared to the Jews that "God the LORD" — the eternally self-existing One — weaved together the heavens and stretched them like a canopy over the whole earth (42:5). The seraphim had announced in Isaiah's hearing that "The whole earth is full of His glory" (6:3), so Isaiah was able to declare with deep conviction that God created life and sustained it by "giv[ing] breath to the people on [the earth] / And spirit to those who walk in it" (42:5). God's concern for humanity, His desire to reveal Himself and dwell with them, led Him to bestow a calling (42:6). The call was certain because of the faithfulness of the Caller — "I . . . the LORD." The call was characteristic, in keeping with God's "righteousness" or holiness. And the call was confident because God promised His presence and protection to the one called. What was the call? To carry "a light to the nations" (42:6). Isaiah was writing to the Hebrews, the chosen people, telling them that God's plan was not that they be the single repository of the truth: they were to shine God's light to *everyone*. As followers of Christ, we have also been given this calling.

How many times is the first person pronoun "I" used in Isaiah 42:6? _____

What conclusion(s) would you draw from the repetition of "I" in Isaiah 42:6?

_____

_____

_____

_____

Those who answer the call of God, who become His torchbearers, are to enlighten "the nations," or as the Scripture specifies, enlighten those with "blind eyes," "prisoners [in] the dungeon / And those who dwell in darkness" (Isaiah 42:7). The dark and dank spiritual dungeon in which humanity finds itself is one of its own making. But God sends us to kick in the doors of humanity's dungeon and bring the freeing light of truth into the lives of those therein.

Do you know people locked in a dark spiritual dungeon? Who?

_____

_____

_____

_____

_____

Do you believe God has called you to be "a light" to those in darkness? Explain.

_____

_____

_____

_____

_____

What have you done recently to bring the light to those in darkness?

_____

_____

_____

_____

We who are called to carry God's light can become smug, especially if, as we answer the call, God frees spiritual prisoners from their sin. God's calling is a high one and a privilege—it's easy to subtly slip into the sin of self-conceit, thinking we are the ones worthy of honor. So God gives us a strong reminder. "I am the LORD, that is My name" (Isaiah 42:8). He reminds us He is the same God who created the heavens and the earth, who gives and sustains life. And then literally and emphatically He declares, "I will not give My glory to another" (42:8).

The juxtaposition of God's personal, covenant-making name— *Yahweh*, which we read as "LORD" and which reveals His essential character—and His declaration to keep His glory to Himself points a finger into our sternum as to how jealously God protects His glory. God's glory reveals His character, and He does not share His glory with anyone, including "graven images," or idols, which cannot do what He can do.

An Example We Should Always Remember

Light-bearers should always remember God's declaration in
Isaiah 42:8 because nothing is more repugnant to God than the idolatry of self-conceit. How easy it is for us to fall into the trap of pride
and to attempt to steal the glory that belongs only to our great God, as
the king we're about to meet tragically illustrates.

 Skim 2 Chronicles 26:1–15.

Everyone admired King Uzziah, even at the young age of 16,
because he followed the Lord and diligently sought God's wisdom
through the sage advice of Zechariah (2 Chronicles 26:1–5). As long
as Uzziah "sought the LORD, God prospered him" (26:5).

**Read each of the following verses from 2 Chronicles 26 and note
how God prospered Uzziah.**

26:6–7

_____

_____

_____

26:9–10

_____

_____

_____

26:11–15

_____

_____

_____

Armies marched in battle array at the command of his voice. Buildings rose from the dust at the wave of his hand. Foreign governments paid tribute at the power of his presence. God did all of this for Uzziah, and Uzziah became famous worldwide (2 Chronicles 26:8, 15). And then . . .

Everything changed. Power, prestige, wealth, renown—how "marvelously helped" by God he was . . . "until he was strong" (26:15). Slowly, imperceptibly, Uzziah began to seek Zechariah's counsel less and less often. Little by little, drip by drip, he drank in his own fame. He no longer needed God's help; he was the great Uzziah—commander of armies and builder of buildings! But the daily dripping of pride became a river in his soul, carving a canyon of weak character that ended in corruption.

 Read 2 Chronicles 26:16–23.

Uzziah went too far. He resembled some contemporary politicians who think that they are above the rules and so vote themselves pay raises while failing to pay taxes, creating a public scandal. "When [Uzziah] became strong, his heart was so proud that he acted corruptly" (26:16).

Uzziah's vanity, his self-conceit, led him to the one place he should never have gone—to walk floors his feet should never have trod. Seeing the king enter the sacred space of the sanctuary with a censer in his hand, Azariah and eighty courageous priests rushed after Uzziah—the commander of a 307,500-man army (26:13)—and demanded he leave the temple immediately. They knew his intentions.

Who had the right to burn incense before the Lord, according to Exodus 30:7–8 and 2 Chronicles 26:18?

_____

_____

_____

Uzziah's pride convinced him that his authority and rule included the Lord's temple. By entering the sanctuary, Uzziah disregarded the specific and sacred Law of God and essentially anointed himself as priest (2 Chronicles 26:17–18). Then, when challenged by the men of God, the king, in his madness, became "enraged" (26:19). The word carries the idea of a dark and ominous storm cloud covering one's countenance, threatening to violently break forth at any moment.[4]

Read 2 Chronicles 26:19–23 and, in your own words, relate what happened to Uzziah.

_____

_____

_____

_____

_____

_____

Uzziah brazenly usurped God's decree and foolishly tried to take that which belongs only to God—His glory. For this the young man who began with such promise, so blessed by God, would end his days as a man nobody respected, as an outcast of society, as a king with a crooked crown.

STARTING YOUR JOURNEY

The Lord has made it clear: "I will not give My glory to another" (Isaiah 42:8), not even to one whom the Lord appointed king over His people. Our God is a jealous God, protecting what belongs only to Him. Lest we, like Uzziah, fall into the trap of vainglory in our lives and areas of responsibility, we should mark well these five warnings.

First, *beware when greater battles are fought within than without.* These include battles fought for power, position, or money.

Second, and related to the first, *beware when more attention falls on one who is building his or her own kingdom instead of the Lord's.* When our own or someone else's image or agenda becomes more important than what God wants, then we've fallen into the sin of stealing God's glory.

Third, *beware when the Lord's help is no longer considered essential.* If we believe we no longer need God's guidance from the Scriptures or prayer in order to minister, to lead a family, or to live the Christian life, we are walking on a slippery slope.

Fourth, *beware when reproofs and warnings are resisted instead of respected.* God sends wise and godly people into our lives, as He did for Uzziah. When we cease listening to them we are in danger of falling, as Uzziah did.

Finally, *beware when the consequences of sin no longer bring fear.* When we play with the matches of sin, it is easy to be reckless when the consequences appear delayed. But losing the fear of burning ourselves is a sure step in setting a torch that will scorch our souls.

Each of these warnings is another way of saying beware of pride. It robs God of His rightful place in our lives; it seeks to steal His glory.

Write Proverbs 16:18 in your own words.

_____

_____

_____

_____

_____

How prideful are you?

	Rate Yourself	Have Someone Else Rate You
Not Very		
Somewhat		
Very		

Be cautious: even what looks to others like humility can be pride. Many think that having a humble spirit means having a low sense of self-worth. Yet when we demean ourselves, we're actually saying, "I know more about my true value than God does." And in the end, that's pride too! It defies the truth of your value that's clearly stated in His Word.

What do you think God's attitude is toward proud people?

_____

_____

_____

_____

_____

How does your answer above compare with James 4:6?

_____

_____

_____

_____

_____

What should you do about your pride? What will God do if you take that kind of action? Read 1 Peter 5:6 to find out.

_____

_____

_____

_____

_____

❧

Vainglory is an ugly vice, for it can see nothing but its own distorted reflection. It is the futile attempt to make oneself into one's own god, seeking one's own good and goal, finding meaning only in oneself. It is John Quincy Adams lording his education over his contemporaries. It is Uzziah assuming a role that was never his. It is Hamlet pretending to be Shakespeare. But Hamlet isn't Shakespeare; Hamlet simply reflects the glory of Shakespeare. And we, like Hamlet, reflect the glory of our Maker, the glory that belongs to God alone. He does not share His glory with another.

> Now . . . to the only God our Savior, through Jesus Christ our Lord, be glory, majesty, dominion and authority, before all time and now and forever. Amen. (Jude 1:24–25)

Lesson Two

The Holiness of God
Isaiah 6:1–8

 THE HEART OF THE MATTER
What comes to your mind when you think about God?
Whatever thoughts enter your mind, chances are they say
more about you than they do about God.

Both in the church and in society, it's fashionable to prefer a god
who is predictable, not one of mystery; a god who is comfortable, not
one who makes us shudder; a god who is a little holier than humans,
but not too holy. In short, we want a god like us, only better. How
squalid such thoughts are, for our God is none of these things. In
His unique otherness, our God graciously reveals the beauty of His
holiness, by which we see the ugliness of our wretchedness and, yet,
also find the encouragement to be holy as He is.

 DISCOVERING THE WAY
Few writers, in wrestling with how to communicate truth,
have written about God's character with more penetrating
eloquence than A. W. Tozer. In the early 1960s, in what
many consider his *magnum opus*, *The Knowledge of the Holy*, Tozer
wrote:

> It is my opinion that the Christian conception of
> God . . . is so decadent [marked by decay] as to be
> utterly beneath the dignity of the Most High God and
> actually to constitute for professed believers some-
> thing amounting to a moral calamity. . . .

13

> . . . And for this we are now paying a too heavy
> price in the secularization of our religion and the
> decay of our inner lives.[1]

We may wish that things had improved in our thinking since that time, but they have not. In fact, our thinking about God is perhaps more decadent. We simply are not "qualified to appreciate the holiness of God."[2] Something new, something startling, must take place in our minds and souls to awaken us to the beauty of God's holiness. Then and only then will we find decay turn to life.

What comes to your mind when you think about God?

Basically, to be "holy" means "to be set apart." What comes to your mind when you think about God's holiness?

Revisiting an Ancient Temple

Not since the days of Solomon had Judah known a king like Uzziah. Popular and powerful, Uzziah began his reign under the blessings of God. But, as we learned in lesson 1, as the years passed, his power and popularity rotted his commitment to the Lord until, in his pride, Uzziah spat upon God's holiness by vainly attempting to steal the glory of God. Uzziah's punishment was leprosy, and he was buried without honor (see 2 Chronicles 26:5–21).

In the year that Uzziah died (739 BC), in the city of Jerusalem, a distraught man of noble birth, possibly a priest, encountered the holy God—an encounter that would change his life forever.

Read Isaiah 6:1–4.

Theologians debate whether Isaiah saw his vision in the physical temple in Jerusalem or whether he was transported in his vision to God's throne room in heaven. Regardless, Isaiah immediately beheld the glory of the sovereign Lord of creation. God, as the "lofty and exalted" One in Isaiah's vision, was transcendent—outside and above creation, not confined to time and space but beyond them—holding the universe and all it contains in the palm of His hand, as it were. But more than this, God's royal majesty filled the temple, as His royal robe spilled out from the throne.

Jesus taught that a select group of people would see the face of God. Who are they, according to Matthew 5:8?

_____

_____

_____

Isaiah saw more than the Lord in his vision; he also saw angels encircling God's throne (Isaiah 6:2). Described only in Isaiah 6:2 and 6:6, these six-winged "seraphim," meaning "fiery ones,"[3] ministered with burning zeal in their worship of God and in the service of purification, as we'll see. With two wings, Isaiah wrote, the seraphim continually hide their faces in humility before God, never once peeking a glance at His glory. With two wings they cover their feet in the exalted presence of God, never to treat Him with flippant familiarity. And with two wings they fly in service to God, ever ready at the command of the Lord.

The seraphim's ministry is to proclaim the glory and holiness of God. Isaiah's experience of hearing the seraphim calling out one to another—"Holy, Holy, Holy" (6:3)—was significant. For God to express His transcendence to Isaiah, He didn't have to use words, He just had to show up. But God knows it is dangerous for a person to try to understand His character based on raw experience alone. He introduced, therefore, a cognitive and rational element into Isaiah's vision, because words interpret spiritual experiences.

The "Holy, Holy, Holy" in the seraphim's song does not represent the number of seraphim in the angelic choir, though it may represent the Trinity of Father, Son, and Holy Spirit. It is a literary device called a *trisagion*, used to highlight a strong superlative. The description of God as thrice holy left no doubt in Isaiah's mind, and should leave no doubt in ours, that God is *the only* holy One.

Expounding on the concept of God's holiness, Tozer wrote:

> We cannot grasp the true meaning of the divine holiness by thinking of someone or something very pure and then raising the concept to the highest degree we are capable of. God's holiness is not simply the best we know infinitely bettered. We know nothing like the divine holiness. It stands apart, unique, unapproachable, incomprehensible and unattainable. The natural man is blind to it. He may fear God's power and admire His wisdom, but His holiness he cannot even imagine.[4]

To their song, the seraphim added to their antiphonal praise "The whole earth is full of His glory" (Isaiah 6:3). It was too much for Isaiah. The foundation of the temple shook violently at the sound of the seraphim's voices, causing Isaiah to cower on the threshold. Smoke from the altar of incense, introducing the sense of smell into Isaiah's already overloaded senses, filled the temple (6:4).

Rediscovering the Forgotten Truth

As he experienced the holiness of God, Isaiah's attention shifted from the morally pure (God) to the morally impure (himself).

Read Isaiah 6:5–8.

Excruciatingly aware of his moral filth under the spotlight of God's holiness, Isaiah cried: "Woe is me, for I am ruined!" (Isaiah 6:5). The pronouncement of "woe" was sometimes used by prophets to declare divine judgment (see Matthew 23:13–33). Here Isaiah brought the judgment of God down upon his own head. Why such intense despair? Under the searing heat of God's holiness, Isaiah came to understand who he really was, a "man of unclean lips" living "among a people of unclean lips" (Isaiah 6:5).

"Profanity," it has been said, "is the parlance of fools." Whether or not Isaiah was a fool before entering the temple, in the presence of the Lord he was wise enough to confess his sin. Then, as if Isaiah's confession caused a hush to descend on the temple, one of the fiery angels flew to Isaiah and touched his lips with a burning ember from God's holy altar (6:6–7). Psssss . . . the red-hot coal met the moisture of Isaiah's lips and in the fire of God's righteousness, unrighteousness was consumed—"your iniquity is taken away and your sin is forgiven" (6:7). What grace!

Because God is holy, He has made holiness the moral imperative of His creation. Anything that is unholy must be purified. It is no accident, then, that God's holiness is associated with fire throughout the Bible.

In each of the passages below, what is the relationship between fire and God's holiness?

Exodus 3:1–6

_____

_____

_____

_____

Leviticus 10:1–2

_____

_____

_____

_____

Numbers 11:1–2

_____

_____

_____

_____

1 Kings 18:24, 38

_____

_____

_____

_____

What did you discover about God or about holiness through this exercise?

_____

_____

_____

_____

It is by God's grace that we are not destroyed under the heat of His holiness. It is by God's grace that He chooses to forgive us. God desires to fellowship with people (see Hosea 11:8–11; 2 Peter 3:9), but He will not when sin and iniquity reside within our hearts. It is for us, the unholy, when confronted with the holiness of God to confess and have our sins seared from our lives.

It was only after forgiveness that Isaiah was ready to hear the voice of God and respond to His call. God's greatness and mercy compels Him to stoop to sinners, like Isaiah, and ask: "Whom shall I send, and who will go for Us?" (Isaiah 6:8). Isaiah's response, "Here am I," is a confession of "Scrutinize me, I have nothing to hide" and a contribution of "What can I do? Send me."

"Such a grateful offering of themselves," one commentator wrote, "is always the cry of those who have received God's grace after they have given up hope of ever being acceptable to God."[5] Isaiah found grace in God's holiness and was acceptable to Him for the rest of his life, being a "sent one" to the kingdom of Judah for almost sixty years.

STARTING YOUR JOURNEY

Learning about the holiness of God should not be another thing to check off our theological list of things to know about Him. Rather, it should compel us to action. Knowledge of God's holiness means that as He is separate from sin, so our lives are to be set apart from sin (see 1 Peter 1:15–16). We are to live wholesomely in an unwholesome world, be authentic in an inauthentic world, and speak the truth in a "truthless" world. And the place to start is in our minds, our mouths, and our morals.

In our minds we must counteract our depravity with godly thoughts. As our minds go, so go our lives.

What does Romans 12:2 command us to do?

_____

_____

_____

Be creative; what are some ways you can renew your mind and thereby counteract thoughts of sinfulness? (See Psalm 119:9–11 for one hint.)

_____

_____

_____

From our mouths we should be free from all unwholesome words. All of us have said things, whether profanity or inappropriate jokes or biting put-downs, that are not becoming of God's children. Let's stop that!

Have you in the past or do you currently struggle with profanity? If so, why do you think that is?

_____

_____

_____

What does Ephesians 5:4 command us not to do in our conversation?

_____

_____

_____

What impact do you think profanity has on a Christian's testimony or reputation?

_____

_____

_____

Instead of profanity, especially in the presence of non-Christians, what did Paul encourage in Colossians 4:6?

_____

_____

_____

_____

In our morals we need to be cleansed from every compromise. In the worlds of business, politics, or dispute resolution, compromise may be appropriate, but the compromise of character is intolerable.

In what areas do you find it most tempting to compromise?

Truth telling (lying or hiding the truth)	
Sexual purity (fornication)	
Honest dealings (cheating)	
Proper payment (stealing)	
Hard work (laziness)	

Are there other areas not listed in which you're tempted to compromise?

_____

_____

_____

_____

_____

For the areas you checked or listed, look in your Bible's concordance—an alphabetical list of words found in the Bible—and find at least one passage of Scripture addressing that moral issue. Write those passages below or on a note card.

_____

_____

_____

_____

_____

_____

Now, commit yourself to memorizing those passages over the next few weeks.

Does purifying your mind, mouth, and morals seem overwhelming and impossible? According to Philippians 2:12–13 and Hebrews 13:20–21, who is responsible for making changes? What is your part?

_____

_____

_____

_____

❧

The Knowledge of the Holy gives us one more challenge.

> Wherever God appeared to men in Bible times the results were the same—an overwhelming sense of terror and dismay, a wrenching sensation of sinfulness and guilt. When God spoke, Abram stretched himself

upon the ground to listen. When Moses saw the Lord in the burning bush, he hid his face in fear to look upon God. Isaiah's vision of God wrung from him the cry, "Woe is me!" and the confession, "I am undone; because I am a man of unclean lips." . . .

These experiences show that a vision of the divine transcendence soon ends all controversy between the man and his God. The fight goes out of the man and he is ready with the conquered Saul to ask meekly, "Lord, what wilt thou have me to do?"[6]

And so it is for all who see the holiness of God, for those who have eyes to see.

Lesson Three

The Love of God
Selected Scriptures

THE HEART OF THE MATTER

Love is the best known but least understood of God's attributes. Many believe His love—as demonstrated in His patience, mercy, and forgiveness—nullifies His righteousness, justice, and holiness. This popular notion of God, as if He were a benign, aging grandfather, sitting passively in heaven and devoid of any real displeasure over sin, cheapens God's love. To peek into God's loving heart is to discover His other attributes as well. Embracing an accurate understanding of God's love for us, as verified through the death and resurrection of His Son, Jesus, is especially important for those first coming to grips with God's attributes.

DISCOVERING THE WAY

First John 4:8 states unequivocally: "God is love." Wrapping our minds around this profound truth requires us to stretch our thinking, because so many of us misunderstand both who God is and what love is. Some believe that love is a feeling that you feel when you feel a feeling that you've never felt before. These folks fall in love with the romantic view of love—what Augustine called being "in love with love." [1] But love is much more than warm regard for another person. It involves a host of other things. For instance, it involves limits. Wives do not send their husbands off on business trips with "blank checks" to sin, implying: "Do anything you want, Sweetheart, because I love you." Nonsense! Wives expect fidelity in their husbands, borne out of love for their wives. Love also requires mutual respect, patience, wisdom, generosity, forgiveness, and more. And, in order for love to be perceived and received, it must be demonstrated. Contrary to popular sentiments, the biblical idea of love is one of volition and action. And no one demonstrates this kind of love greater than God our Father through Jesus His Son.

How can you tell if someone loves you? What does this person do; how does he or she act? What would you think of someone who said he or she loved you but never did any of these things?

_____

_____

_____

_____

All loving relationships involve conflict. According to Romans 5:8, what is God's natural inclination to wrongs done to Him? How did He demonstrate that inclination?

_____

_____

_____

_____

God Is What?

God personifies unconditional love; love permeates who He is and everything He does. His love is spontaneous, sacrificial, and consistent.

 Read 1 John 4:7–8, 16.

Many have wrongly inferred that John conveyed the singular essence of God in three simple words—"God is love." This is heresy because it is idolatry. Love is not all of who God is. As A. W. Tozer so carefully wrote, "If love is equal to God then God is only equal to love, and God and love are identical. Thus we destroy the concept of personality in God and deny outright all His attributes save one, and that one we substitute for God."[2] If love were the essence of God, and God is the only One worthy of our worship, then we must commit the sin of being "in love with love" . . . which is idolatry. Scripture teaches that God is more than love.

Match the following attributes of God with the correct Scripture. (If you're unsure, please see the answers on page 142.)

	Attribute		Scripture
_G_ 1.	All-Knowing (Omniscient)	A.	Jeremiah 10:10
_E_ 2.	All-Powerful (Omnipotent)	B.	Luke 18:19
_J_ 3.	Everywhere Present (Omnipresent)	C.	Psalm 145:8–9
_H_ 4.	Wise	D.	Exodus 34:6
_B_ 5.	Good	E.	Luke 1:37
_I_ 6.	Faithful	F.	Isaiah 6:3
_A_ 7.	True	G.	1 John 3:20
_DE_ 8.	Gracious	H.	Romans 11:33–34
_F_ 9.	Holy	I.	Deuteronomy 7:9
_C_ 10.	Merciful/Compassionate	J.	Psalm 139:7–10

Love cannot be the essence of God because, using exactly the same phrasing, John wrote earlier about God's purity when he said, "God is Light" (1 John 1:5). Not a speck of darkness resides in God; not a hint or particle of unholiness or impurity dwells in Him. And as God is the quintessence of love, so He is the quintessence of holiness. He is 100 percent love and 100 percent holy at the same time. In fact, all of God's attributes—the truth of His character—are equally divine and undiminished; none is greater than another.

God's love must never be separated from His other characteristics. While His love is unconditional, it is not uncritical. We see this principle at work in everyday relationships.

 Read Hebrews 12:5–11.

Loving mothers and fathers discipline their children; they don't allow the house to turn into a barrel of monkeys, where unruly urchins reign in chaos. Undisciplined children are unloved children and are seen, in the words of Hebrews, as "illegitimate" (Hebrews 12:8). God disciplines us because He is holy and because He loves us too much to allow us to live our lives in sin. In that regard, He is our loving heavenly Father.

According to Hebrews 12:10, what is the difference between how our earthly parents disciplined us and how God disciplines us?

Earthly parents:

_____

_____

_____

Heavenly Father:

_____

_____

_____

What is the result of God's discipline, according to Hebrews 12:10–11?

_____

_____

_____

_____

God's Love in the Old and New Testaments

Talking about God's love in theory is useful, but seeing examples of God's love in action gives His love life. Fortunately, both the Old and New Testaments are chock-full of illustrations.

 DIGGING DEEPER
A God with Two Faces?
Some have observed that God as He revealed Himself in the Old Testament is One of stern justice and capricious wrath, bordering on the thin edge of madness, while God as He revealed Himself in the New Testament is loving and merciful, a doddering grandfatherly type who smiles a lot but doesn't quite know why. Both are extreme distortions of the popular view that God is inconsistent or hasn't revealed Himself consistently in Scripture. Such a notion renders God as schizophrenic.

This dual vision of God is not only unbiblical (see Hebrews 13:8), it reduces God to a god (with a lowercase "g") . . . which is to say it reduces Him to no god at all, because it denies His unchanging nature or reduces Him only to a god of our making. The problem lies not in the reality of God but in the perspective of those who cannot see God's love in the Old Testament and His justice in the New Testament. Many have wrongly concluded that love and justice are mutually

Continued on next page

29

Continued from previous page

exclusive. But justice is not the opposite of love (nor is hate), indifference is. (Even hatred recognizes the existence and worth of another, at least worthy of time and negative attention.) Indifference treats another as a nonperson, as nonexistent; justice treats another as worthy of redemption, as worthy of love. Justice may seem a cruel cut, but the cruelest cut is the cut that never comes — that is indifference. God's love is too great not to cut out our sin with the scalpel of justice. He cannot be indifferent and let us die from the cancer of sin.

We may take God as He really is or reject Him on the same basis, but the one opinion not open to us is to create Him as we'd like Him to be. He is and has always been the God of love and justice in both the Old and New Testaments.

 Read Deuteronomy 7:6–8.

With the passing of the former, rebellious generation, Moses reiterated God's commandments to another generation — reminding them of God's sovereign love. "The Lord did not set His love on you nor choose you because you were more in number than any of the peoples . . . but because the Lord loved you" (Deuteronomy 7:7–8). Like a parent answering a child's inquiry of "why," God loved Israel "because." Because God loved Israel, He chose Israel.

Read Jeremiah 31:3. What does this verse say about God's love?

_____

_____

_____

_____

What is implied in Jeremiah 31:3 as to why God chose to love Israel?

_____

_____

Read John 3:14–16.

In these famous verses we see the extent of God's love. Who of us would willingly send our sons or daughters to a certain death for the salvation of ungrateful and sinful people? God did. And because He did, those who believe in Jesus will have eternal life. What great love that is!

Earlier we read that "while we were yet sinners, Christ died for us" (Romans 5:8). But what does it mean to be a sinner? Read Romans 3:10–18 and write down Paul's definition.

_____

_____

_____

_____

_____

_____

Now circle any descriptions that are true of you.

Even if you circled only one description in the list, then you must agree that you are a _____.

Jesus's Parable Illustrates the Extent of God's Love

It is a shameful thing to admit you are a sinner. So shameful for some that they cannot believe God could ever love them. Yet there is hope. As the parable of the prodigal son illustrates and as Paul's grand declaration proves, God's love reaches those in the miry muck of sin and makes them clean and whole.

 Read Luke 15:11–24.

This parable really shouldn't be called the prodigal son but the loving father, because as the boy was away squandering his inheritance on riotous living, his father kept a daily vigil, watching for his son's return (see Luke 15:20). The climax of the story comes in verses 20–24. Seeing his son stumble up the road, the father jumped from his porch, ran to him, and showered his swine-smelling son with kisses. The boy tried to confess his sin, but the father, elated with unspeakable joy, interrupted him and called his servants to

> "bring a clean set of clothes and dress him. Put the family ring on his finger and sandals on his feet. Then get a grain-fed heifer and roast it. We're going to feast! We're going to have a wonderful time! My son is here—given up for dead and now alive! Given up for lost and now found!" (Luke 15:22–24 MSG)

Read the story of the loving father again. Do you identify with the prodigal son? Have you ever run away, either literally or through some other rebellion, and returned to ask forgiveness of your earthly parents? If so, what was their response?

_____

_____

_____

_____

_____

If you decided to return to God after a long absence in the pigsty of sin, do you think God would respond to you as your earthly parents did or as the father in the story did? Explain.

_____

_____

_____

_____

_____

 Read Romans 8:31–39.

If the story of the loving father is the greatest illustration of God's love, then Paul's words in Romans 8:31–39 are the triumphant declaration of God's love. With God on our side, who can oppose us? If He gave us His most precious gift, His Son, will He withhold any good from us? Who can charge or condemn us? God is the judge and Jesus is the redeemer who prays for us. Nothing, absolutely nothing, can separate us from God's great love!

 STARTING YOUR JOURNEY
The greatest story of God's love may be the parable of the loving father, and the greatest statement may be in Romans 8, but the greatest demonstration of His love is the death and resurrection of His Son, Jesus Christ.

God's Love Demonstrated for All

The world is divided into two groups. One group knows the intimacy of God's love because, in faith, they believe that Christ reconciled them to the Father by removing their sin when He died on the cross and that Christ transferred everlasting life to them when He rose from the grave. The other group knows nothing of God's intimate love because they refuse to believe.

If you are a believer in Christ but you tend to doubt God's love for you, reread Romans 8:35–39 and write in it your own words.

_____

_____

_____

_____

_____

_____

Copy what you wrote above onto a 3-inch by 5-inch card and carry it with you this week as a reminder of God's love for you.

If you have not yet made a decision to follow Christ and you desire to know the intimacy of God's love, read Romans 10:9–10 and answer the following questions.

What must you confess?

_____

_____

_____

_____

What must you believe?

_____

_____

_____

_____

What is the result?

_____

_____

_____

_____

Now read Ephesians 2:8–9. What is and what isn't the basis of salvation?

The basis of salvation:

_____

_____

_____

_____

Not the basis of salvation:

_____

_____

_____

_____

If you want to know more about the extent of God's love for you, read "How to Begin a Relationship with God" on page 133 of this Bible Companion.

How does God's method for salvation through Christ exhibit His love without denying His other attributes?

_____

_____

_____

_____

❦

> "This is how much God loved the world: He gave his Son, his one and only Son. And this is why: so that no one need be destroyed; by believing in him, anyone can have a whole and lasting life." (John 3:16 MSG)

To people perishing in their ignorance of the reality of God, such a message of love seems inconceivable. They believe their sin is too great and God, though affable, is too weak to do much about it. How sadly incorrect that view is. God's love is greater and tougher than our sin. His is a love so great that He sent His own Son to die on a cruel cross, just to win the hearts of humanity . . . including yours. No greater love than that exists!

Lesson Four

The Grace of God
2 Samuel 9:1–13

THE HEART OF THE MATTER

Some Bible words have been handled and mishandled for so long they have become shopworn and of little interest to anyone. Not so with the word *grace*; it still retains its luster and mystery. Perhaps this is so because grace can never be earned or rewarded, never demanded. Grace is a gift. It is grace to taste an ice-cream cone, grace to walk in a park, grace to hear a child's coo, grace to look into the face of a beloved, grace to have a soul cleansed by the death of Christ . . . each one, a gift of grace. Such grace is given to the spiritually disabled. Should not those who have received it extend the same grace to others, especially those with physical and emotional disabilities?

DISCOVERING THE WAY

In 1817, Mary Wollstonecraft Shelley completed what has become a classic horror novel—*Frankenstein*. The monster in the story is often mistakenly called Frankenstein but, actually, he has no name, which adds to his isolation and alienation from the world of humans into which he was created. His inhuman deeds, his awkwardness, and his appearance make him an outcast from humanity, eliciting from him an eloquent cry at the end of the novel: "I, the miserable and the abandoned, am an abortion, to be spurned at, and kicked, and trampled on." [1]

Too many real people have known the fictional monster's plight. Deformed spiritually, emotionally, or physically, they have been treated by others as outcasts and objects of misshapen curiosity when what they've needed is grace. What they need is a voice that whispers to their pain and disfigurement, "You are accepted."

How would you define *grace*?

_____

_____

_____

_____

_____

Grace Defined

When God loves, grace follows. As we take a deeper look at God's grace, let's first define it.

 Read Romans 5:6, 8, 10.

Few have offered a better definition of grace than A. W. Tozer: "Grace is the good pleasure of God that inclines Him to bestow benefits upon the undeserving."[2] In a divine act, apart from anything in us—apart from any goodness, effort, or attempts to win God's favor—God stoops from His heavenly realm and whispers to us, "You are accepted."

All of us are undeserving of God's grace because, apart from Him, all of us are sinful, thickheaded, pursuers of selfish pleasures, evil at heart, and worthy to be thrown on the trash heap because of our sin (see Romans 3:10–12).

In the columns, write down the one- or two-word description of who we are and what God has done for us.

Romans 5	Description of Humans	God's Actions
verse 6		
verse 8		
verse 10		

Another word for God's actions is: _____

Some mistakenly believe that the old saying "God helps those who help themselves" is found in the Bible. Look far and wide, high and low, and you'll never find that pithy axiom anywhere in the Scriptures because it isn't true. We can't help ourselves; we are "helpless," "sinners," and "enemies." We are, to put it bluntly, rotten to the core! Our rottenness began the day of our conception. David said, "in sin my mother conceived me" (Psalm 51:5), meaning that from the moment of physical and spiritual formation he was a sinner.

We are sinners from birth. How can such a radical idea be explained?

 Read Romans 5:12, 19–20.

Serving as humanity's official head, Adam sinned in the garden of Eden (see Genesis 3:6–12), and it infected every person with the deadly disease of sin. When he sinned, we sinned. Like a plague, sin spread throughout the human race, leaving physical and spiritual corpses in its wake. The terrible truth of what is known as "original sin" and its consequences are constantly on display and in contradiction to God's holy standard, His Law, articulated in the first five books of the

Bible. Paul wrote that "The Law came in so that the transgression would increase" (Romans 5:20). The Law points out our sin so we are without excuse as sinners (see 5:13), but the Law also serves as the black backdrop to show the brilliance of the diamond of grace.

If sin came through "one man," Adam (Romans 5:12, 19), what did Christ do on our behalf, according to Romans 5:19?

We were made sinners so that
by Christ we were made
righteous.

If sin increased because of the Law, what does God's grace do in response, according to Romans 5:20?

Where grace abounded, grace
abounded more.

Grace Proclaimed

The Law demands "Do this . . . and live," but it makes no provision for carrying out its commands. People were unable to live up to it. What we needed was something more, something better; what we need is grace. God gave us just such a gift, and He proclaims it in His Word.

Read John 1:1–5, 14–17.

In his gospel, John proclaimed divine grace by introducing the Divine Man, Jesus. Calling Him "the Word," this passage teaches that Jesus, as God, existed before there was time (John 1:1–2). He created time and the universe (1:3; see Colossians 1:16), and all things live because He is life and "Light" (John 1:4–5).

As the great creator God, Jesus could have stayed aloof from the sinfulness of humanity, like some mythical Greek deity living removed on Mount Olympus. Jesus had a better way. He chose to leave His heavenly throne and live among humanity; He moved into our very neighborhood where we saw His "glory," the glory of One "full of grace and truth" (1:14). John the Baptist "testified about Him" (1:15), but John the apostle lived with Him and can rightfully say that "We all live off his generous bounty, gift after gift after gift" (1:16 MSG). What grace! The Law may have come through the great man Moses, but the gift of grace and truth are found in none other than the great Divine Man, Jesus Christ (1:17).

 Read Ephesians 2:8–9.

The apostle Paul proclaimed grace through the preaching of salvation. We who are dead in our sins (Ephesians 2:1) have no means of saving ourselves, not even through the multiplication of good deeds (2:9). Therefore, as a free gift, God gives us grace and faith (2:8). This is the good news, the reason why Jesus moved into our neighborhood, bringing with Him eternal life.

Grace Illustrated

Spiritually speaking, we are all disabled, all impaired in our hearts, incapable of moving toward God. Were it not for grace, we would all be like Frankenstein's monster, spiritually miserable and abandoned. Many of us feel not only spiritually spurned but socially spurned because we live with actual physical, mental, or emotional disabilities. For those people, the biblical account of Mephibosheth hits home in a special way.

Read 2 Samuel 9:1–4.

For years David had run like a common criminal, living in hide-outs in the desert as Israel's King Saul sought his life. But some time after the deaths of Saul and his son Jonathan, David became king over Israel. Establishing the political and religious capital at Jerusalem (2 Samuel 5:6–6:23), David settled in his cedar-paneled palace "and the Lord [gave] him rest on every side from all his enemies" (7:1). While there, resting in his luxurious home, David remembered the promise he had made years before to Jonathan, his good friend (see 1 Samuel 20:14–16).

Prompted by grace, David asked whether any members of Jonathan's family were alive; David wanted to show them "kindness" (2 Samuel 9:1). The word is *chesed*—"goodness" or "favors" often "extended to the lowly, needy and miserable."[3] He wanted to give grace to a member of Jonathan's family. None of David's advisors knew the answer to his question, but they knew of a man who might know: Ziba "a servant of the house of Saul" (9:2). Asking Ziba if there was anyone to whom David could show grace, Ziba said, "There is still a son of Jonathan who is crippled in both feet" (9:3).

Without hesitation, David asked, "Where is he?" "He is . . . in Lo-debar," Ziba answered (9:4). And not expecting grace or deserving it, the crippled son of Jonathan, a nobody from no place, was on the cusp of receiving grace beyond measure.

 Read 2 Samuel 9:5–13.

Surely, being a descendant of the former king, Mephibosheth must have expected harsh treatment or even death from the ruler of the new regime. But he received something entirely different. David's amazing gift of grace to Mephibosheth is analogous to God's gift of grace to us. In fact, there are six analogies we can discover from this story.

First, *as David extended his love to a nobody, so God extends His love to us.* Mephibosheth was a nobody living in no place; he had nothing to offer the king. But David, out of grace and because of a promise made, had Mephibosheth brought to his palace (9:5).

Second, *as David sought and found Mephibosheth, so God seeks and finds us.* Writing about his early life, C. S. Lewis said his search for God was equivalent to "the mouse's search for the cat."[4] This was the case with Mephibosheth—only he wasn't searching for David, but David was searching for him (9:6–7).

Why did Jesus come into the world, according to Luke 19:10?

_____

_____

_____

_____

Why did Jesus come into the world, according to Luke 5:31–32?

_____

_____

_____

_____

Who are the "sick" and the "lost"?

_____

_____

_____

_____

Third, *as David restored Mephibosheth to a place of honor, so God has done for us.* Mephibosheth lost everything when David became king, but David, in grace, restored it all (2 Samuel 9:7).

Fourth, *as David adopted Mephibosheth into his royal family, so God adopts us.* Mephibosheth couldn't believe it. He saw himself as no better than a dead dog, yet David deeded Saul's land back to Mephibosheth and ordered Ziba and his family to cultivate it for Mephibosheth's benefit. Mephibosheth, for the rest of his days, would dine at the king's table, as if he were one of the king's sons (9:8–13).

For those who come to faith in Christ, what does John 1:12 say they are?

_____

_____

_____

_____

What is implied by the phrase "He gave the right" in John 1:12?

_____

_____

_____

_____

Fifth, *Mephibosheth's disability was a constant reminder of David's grace, as our disability is a reminder of God's grace.* In an instant, the nobody from no place became a somebody in a great place, but his feet were still disfigured: "Now he was lame in both feet" (2 Samuel 9:13). Grace doesn't change the reality of disabilities, yet it whispers, "You are accepted."

Sixth, *when Mephibosheth sat down at David's table, there was no status or rank within the family; neither is there in the family of God.* When Mephibosheth sat down next to handsome Absalom, there was no difference in David's eyes because, for him, to look at Mephibosheth was to see the face of Jonathan.

What is the truth that Galatians 3:28 and Colossians 3:11 teach?

_____

_____

_____

_____

_____

What is the implication of that for a Christian's life?

_____

_____

_____

_____

_____

STARTING YOUR JOURNEY

All of us are disabled in one way or another, which is why we need grace. But some of us have disabilities that are more obvious to the world, and we long to be accepted. The tragic truth is that even the family of God is not as accepting or gracious as it should be to people with disabilities. Yet the grace of God teaches this overriding truth: there *because* of the grace of God go I.

Do you know people who, because of a physical, mental, or emotional disability, feel "miserable and . . . abandoned . . . spurned . . . and trampled on"? Write their names here. Do you count yourself among this list?

_____

_____

_____

_____

Paraphrase the six analogies listed in this lesson.

1. _____

2. _____

3. _____

4. _____

5. _____

6. _____

Thinking about those who are disabled and the six analogies, how can you be a "David" to at least one person this week?

_____

_____

_____

_____

Have you been less than gracious to people with physical or mental challenges, maybe dismissive or even cruel? If so, why do you think that is?

_____

_____

_____

_____

Do you need to confess your ill-treatment of people with disabilities? If so, write a confession to the Lord and then contact the individual(s), if appropriate, to make things right.

Gracious Father,

I confess _____

_____

_____

_____

_____

Thank you for accepting me in my sin and extending your grace to me. Amen.

What is the truth of 1 John 1:9?

_____

_____

_____

_____

⁂

Mary Shelley ended her tragic novel with the unnamed and disfigured creature floating upon an ice-raft, "borne away by the waves and lost in darkness and distance." [5] How many in the family of God who suffer with disabilities live a life like that—lost in darkness and distance from the love and grace of the rest of God's children?

May we learn to live like David, to possess the courage to live a life of grace, that we may say to all, regardless of their differences: "You are accepted."

Lesson Five

The Servant Who Came
Philippians 2:5–8

 THE HEART OF THE MATTER

Let's begin with a quiz. Why did Jesus come into the world? What was His purpose? If you said something like, "He came to seek and save those who were lost in their sin" (Luke 19:10), you'd be correct. Congratulations. Here's another question: Why would Jesus do that? Why would Jesus leave His glorious throne in heaven to mingle among sinful humanity and die to save us? What was it that motivated Him? Love? Of course! Grace? Absolutely! Humility? Huh . . . what's humility got to do with it? Everything—humility has everything to do with Jesus's motivation to die for those who are lost in the morass of sin. And, for those He has found and saved already, humility has everything to do with following in Jesus's footsteps.

 DISCOVERING THE WAY

Pagan and unbelieving minds cannot grasp the paradox of divine humility. The ancients believed the gods had little concern for humanity, except to torment human beings for sport or manipulate them for personal gain. The gods, in the ancients' view, were capricious, proud, and dangerous; humility didn't fit the gods' character. The modern-day skeptic believes the one true God is a myth, that He is a void, a nothing, like the darkness of the night. And because God doesn't exist, the skeptic sees no reason for Him to exhibit humility—nothingness cannot embody anything.

But the cross of Christ begs to differ. A study of the character of God cannot deny that rough-hewn piece of wood that symbolizes at least three divine qualities: love, grace, and humility. Divine love stretched out wide its arms to embrace. Divine grace created a link between humanity and God, in which God stoops and says, "You are accepted." Divine humility propelled the God-man, Jesus, to tread a path to the cross.

What comes to your mind when you think of these three truths?

Divine love

_____

_____

_____

_____

Divine grace

_____

_____

_____

_____

Divine humility

_____

_____

_____

_____

Christlikeness in One Word

Search the sayings of Jesus and you'll be hard-pressed to find a clearer autobiographical description of Jesus's character than the pen portrait in Matthew 11:28–29.

 Read Matthew 11:28–29.

In one grand and sweeping statement, Jesus invites everyone burdened and beaten under the load of sin to come to Him and find spiritual refreshment. In *Pilgrim's Progress*, John Bunyan chronicled the journey of Christian, who laid his burden down at the empty cross and the empty grave:

> Thus far did I come laden with my Sin;
> Nor could ought ease the grief that I was in,
> Till I came hither: What a place is this!
> Must here be the beginning of my bliss?
> Must here the Burden fall from off my back?
> Must here the strings that bound it to me crack?
> Blest Cross! blest Sepulchre! blest rather be
> The Man that there was put to Shame for me!¹

What sin(s) is weighing you down and wearying you today?

_____

_____

_____

What have you done to find relief from this burden? How successful has that been?

_____

_____

_____

When we come to Him, Jesus doesn't preach a sermon, doesn't shame us, and doesn't point an accusing finger; He promises rest. Jesus can make such a claim because He is "gentle and humble in heart" (Matthew 11:29). In this verse we find our one-word description of Christlikeness: "humble." The Greek word *tapeinos* here indicates an *attitude* of humility.[2] Jesus came to serve (Mark 10:45); He willingly gave up His station in heaven and took on the attitude of a servant because that was what we needed.

Read John 13:3–5, 12–15. What did Jesus do in these verses? Describe the attitude or mind-set it took to do this.

_____

_____

_____

_____

What is Jesus's command in verses 14 and 15? Why should we obey this command?

_____

_____

_____

_____

What might this command look like when lived out today? How can you put it into practice?

_____

_____

_____

_____

Christ's Humility in Paul's Words

We can come to a deeper understanding of humility as we investigate Jesus's servanthood and His sacrifice for the world as described in the letter to the Philippians. Some of the most eloquent words ever written were penned by Paul as a hymn about divine humility.

 Read Philippians 2:5–8.

The theme of the preceding verses is unity within the body of believers in Christ through the attitude, or mind-set, of humility and unselfish service (Philippians 2:1–4). This sets up Paul's exhortation and the introduction to the hymn: "Think of yourselves the way Christ Jesus thought of himself" (2:5 MSG). What was that way? Using three descriptions, Paul answered that question. These give us crucial insights into divine humility.

First, Paul stated the great truth that Jesus existed before He became a man, in eternity past as the coequal and coeternal God. Theologians call this the pre-incarnation of Christ. Specifically, He "existed in the form of God," the *morphe* of God (2:6). *Morphe* sits at the heart of the word "metamorphosis," but unlike our English word, which indicates a change in form or structure, the Greek word signifies no change. The word used by Paul in verse 6 doesn't point to the physical shape of Jesus but to His "outward expression . . . of his inmost nature," the distinctive essence of His character.[3] And because Paul was talking about God, he was talking about the unchanging essence of deity.

Jesus, distinct from God the Father and God the Holy Spirit in function, is God in form, in essence, and in nature. When Paul wrote that Jesus "did not regard equality with God a thing to be grasped" (2:6), he was not referring to Jesus's divine nature specifically but to the *expression* of His divine nature. Simply put, after weighing the facts, Jesus did not consider that the expression of His divinity was "a treasure to be clutched and retained at all hazards."[4]

Another passage speaking of the pre-incarnation is John 1:1–5. What is John's description of Jesus in these verses, and when does John say Jesus existed?

_____

_____

_____

_____

One outward expression of divinity was the act of creation. What was Jesus's role in creation, according to John 1:3 and Colossians 1:15–17?

_____

_____

_____

_____

Second, because Jesus did not desire to cling to or clutch the expression of His divinity, He willingly "emptied Himself" and took on the *morphe*, the "form," of a human servant (Philippians 2:7). This was the incarnation of Christ—the outward expression of His inmost essence: servanthood.

In exchanging one form of expression for another, Jesus "emptied Himself"; but of what? Some have taught that when Jesus clothed Himself in the skin of human frailty He set aside His divinity. This is not correct. The careful scholar of the ancient-Greek language, Kenneth Wuest, said it well,

> When our Lord set aside the expression of Deity in
> order that He might express Himself as a bondslave,
> He was setting aside His legitimate and natural desires
> and prerogatives as Deity. The basic, natural desire
> and prerogative of Deity is that of being glorified. But

> when Deity sets these aside, it sets its desires aside,
> and setting its desires aside, it sets Self aside.[5]

In taking on human flesh, Jesus didn't become *less* than God; He limited His divine activities and submitted their exercise to the will of God the Father. In other words, He veiled His divinity behind a cloak of humanity.

Third, as if "being found in appearance as a man" (Philippians 2:8), born to lowly, peasant parents wasn't lowly enough, Paul said Jesus lowered Himself even further, in obedience to God the Father, in order to die on a cross like a common criminal. Jesus's crucifixion was disgracefully painful—the worst sort of death for the vilest criminals. Held by nails in the wrists and feet, the one being crucified hung naked from splintered wooden beams, for prying eyes to gawk and mock and birds of prey to terrorize.

Revelation 13:8 says, "All inhabitants of the earth will worship the beast—all whose names have not been written in the book of life belonging to the Lamb that was slain from the creation of the world" (NIV). What are the implications of this in light of Jesus's incarnation and death, according to Philippians 2:7–8?

_____

_____

_____

_____

 DIGGING DEEPER
The Hymn of the Kenosis
Philippians 2:6–11 is an early Christian hymn, which has become commonly known as the *Kenosis*, from the Greek verb, *kenoo*, translated as "emptied" (Philippians 2:7). Though ample evidence suggests that Paul was the hymn writer, scholars

Continued on next page

Continued from previous page

continue to disagree on the authorship of this hymn. Some argue that Paul incorporated the hymn from "a Gentile contemporary . . . who puts into poetic form his praise to Christ in a way similar to his pre-Christian pagan practice of lauding divine heroes."[6] Regardless of whether or not Paul was the author, the truths expressed in the hymn are both inspiring and arresting. In fact, the hymn skillfully captures an early song of praise to the preexistent, earthly, and exalted Christ. Its beauty and simplicity rival anything David wrote in the Psalms and serves as a fitting tribute to our glorious Lord, Jesus Christ!

STARTING YOUR JOURNEY

So horrific was the cross to the ancient mind, the great Roman statesman, Cicero, declared,

> The mere name of the [cross], should be far removed . . . from the persons of Roman citizens,—from their thoughts, and eyes, and ears. For not only the actual fact and endurance of all these things [the executioner and cross], but the bare possibility of being exposed to them,—the expectation, the mere mention of them, even,—is unworthy of a Roman citizen and of a free man. . . . Shall neither our exploits, nor the purity of our past life, nor the honours which you have conferred on us, save us from the scourge, from the hangman's hook, and even from the dread of the [cross]?[7]

No wonder Jesus's death on the cross was a stone of stumbling to Jews and "foolishness" to Greek and Roman minds (1 Corinthians 1:23). This symbol of cruelty and death was beyond humiliating; it was degrading—and Christ, to save that which was lost, freely chose this. The cross is a powerful symbol of Christ's humility and our faith.

Two other older symbols, foreshadowing Christ's cross, illustrate His gentle and humble spirit in His death and in His glorious resurrection. Both are simple, everyday elements: bread and wine.

On the night of the Passover, God commanded the Israelites to paint their doorposts and lintels with lamb's blood and prepare a meal they could eat quickly. Besides a roasted lamb, what did God command them to prepare, according to Exodus 12:8? What does God command in Exodus 12:17, and why does He make this command?

_____

_____

_____

_____

Read Luke 22:19–20 and 1 Corinthians 11:23–25. What does Jesus command in these passages?

_____

_____

_____

_____

How is this command, in the Lord's Supper, similar to God's command during the Exodus?

_____

_____

_____

_____

The bread and wine represent the humility of Christ's death, His obedience "to the point of death, even death on a cross" (Philippians 2:8), but what of His resurrection? What is implied in Luke 22:18?

All of this leads to two critical questions. For those who already follow Christ, are you clean? Are you living a life like Christ's — pure and humble so you can serve others like He served you? And for those who have not come to faith in Christ, why not? Why haven't you humbled yourself, set aside "self," and come to the Humble One who gives rest from sin, the God who humiliated Himself on the cross for you? What is holding you back? Come. Come today.

If you'd like to learn more about finding rest from the burden of your sins, please read "How to Begin a Relationship with God" on page 133 of this Bible Companion.

The little-known and little-celebrated British statesman and social reformer William Wilberforce understood the essence of the Christian faith. "Humility," he wrote, "is . . . the vital principle of Christianity." [8] No one comes to Christ without first humbling himself or herself and admitting his or her need for a Savior; no one continues in Christ without following Christ's example of humble servitude. So whether we look upon the cross or remember Christ in the bread and wine, we are reminded of divine love, divine grace, and divine humility — a humility that wrings from our mouths the heartfelt confession that "Jesus Christ is Lord, to the glory of God the Father" (Philippians 2:11).

Lesson Six

The Cup That He Drank
John 18:1–11

 THE HEART OF THE MATTER
It has been said that the secret to a happy life is learning
how to avoid pain. We certainly live in a day in which
this philosophy holds sway. Ours is a comfort-at-any-
cost, I-want-it-quick-and-easy society; a society that trumpets, "It's
all about me!" Yet, what the world shuns as foolishness, the Lord
embraces as wisdom—the wisdom of pain to turn mere followers of
Christ into true disciples of Christ. Pain is the process God uses for
the living to gain wisdom. Jesus called it "the cup." To Him the cup
was the anguish, humiliation, and torturous death on the cross. To us
it means "taking up our cross" and following Him daily.

 DISCOVERING THE WAY
This is not a comfortable thought but a true one none-
theless: "When God wants to do an impossible task, He
takes an impossible man and crushes him."[1] A. W. Tozer
expressed a similar thought: "It is doubtful whether God can bless a
man greatly until He has hurt him deeply."[2]

A casual reading of these words might lead us to the conclusion
that God is cruel or brutal. Nothing could be further from the truth.
God is not capricious. Out of His great love, He desires to develop
Christians into disciples, but it is not an easy or pain-free process;
like a baby who's cutting useful teeth, there's bound to be pain
involved. "The conversion of a soul is the miracle of a moment,"
the late Alan Redpath said in 1959 at a Dallas Theological Seminary

chapel service, "but the making of a saint is the task of a lifetime." And that always entails suffering.

How would you define these two words, if someone asked you to?

What is a *Christian*?

_____

_____

_____

What is a *disciple*?

_____

_____

_____

On Being a Christian . . . On Becoming a Disciple

Coming to Christ in faith is easy and takes no more than a second to accomplish. Becoming a disciple of Christ, however, is an arduous journey that will never fully be complete in this lifetime. But the journey is worth the taking.

 Read Luke 9:23.

Before we dive into the detail of Jesus's words in Luke 9, review the chart on page 69, which illustrates the progress from unbelief to faith in Christ to becoming His disciple.

Before coming to Christ, all of us were without "excuse" as to the judgment of God (Romans 2:1), were His "enemies" (5:10), and "were dead in [our] trespasses and sins" (Ephesians 2:1). Yet by His great grace and through the exercise of faith (see 2:8), we came, through the cross of Christ, to forgiveness of sins and the salvation of our souls; this is called *conversion*—a "miracle of the moment." As believers in the Lord Jesus Christ, we have been delivered "from the domain of darkness" (Colossians 1:13), have been "born of the Spirit" (John 3:6), and are rightly called "children of God" (1:12). Yet, out of this pool of believers, few commit to the crushing lifestyle of discipleship. Most remain content with a right relationship to God through faith in Jesus Christ—simply being a Christian.

Look back over your definition of a Christian. How does it compare with the one just given in the previous paragraph?

_____

_____

_____

Read the following passages and jot down the important ideas of what it means to be a believer in Christ.

Acts 16:31

_____

_____

1 John 5:11–12

_____

_____

_____

Discipleship entails much more than embracing Christ in faith. A disciple is a believer whose commitment to Christ has grown into a deep desire to obey, regardless of the consequences, the sacrifice, or the cost.

Look back over your definition of a disciple. How does it compare to the one just given?

_____

_____

_____

Discipleship involves renouncing lesser loyalties, loving Christ more than anyone or anything, and submitting our selfish wills in obedience to His will. Discipleship means denying and dying to self, as Jesus taught in Luke 9:23. All believers—past, present, and future—who desire to become Christ's disciples must do three things.

First, *they must deny themselves.* They must learn to say no to their selfish desires and yes to anything Christ demands. In other words, disciples must dethrone themselves and enthrone Christ. Second, *they must take up their crosses every day.* Greater than denial, this is a daily death to self. Disciples must slay stubborn wills and find life in doing His will, every day. Third, *they must follow Him wherever He leads.* Disciples obey no matter the command; they emulate no matter the cost, even if the cost is suffering.

Moving from the realm of the complacent Christian to the domain of the committed Christian will cost you something dear . . . which is why the church produces so few disciples. The way of discipleship is the way of difficulty—but it is also the way of reward.

Read Luke 9:57–62 and answer the following questions.

What is the implication for those who would follow Jesus that the animals of the field have a home but Jesus does not?

_____

_____

_____

What do you think Jesus meant by letting the dead bury
the dead?

_____

_____

_____

What do you think Jesus meant in Luke 9:62?

_____

_____

_____

How would you summarize Jesus's message in 9:57–62?

_____

_____

_____

Being completely honest, are you ready to sign up for Jesus's
discipleship program? Why, or why not?

_____

_____

_____

Jesus Christ Our Lord: The Ideal Example

Jesus is indeed our Master who can command us to deny and die to
self, not only because He is God but because He knew what it meant
to deny and die to His own will.

 Read John 18:1–11.

The context of John 18 is sweeping. Jesus and His disciples had finished the Passover meal in the upper room, where He taught them the humility of the basin and the towel (John 13). From the upper room, through the streets of Jerusalem, Jesus comforted them with what He knew would be some of His final words (John 14–16). And before He crossed over the Kidron Valley to enter the garden at the place called Gethsemane, Jesus prayed for all who would follow Him (John 17). Now, having entered the garden and having endured the brutality of His agonizing prayer (Mark 14:32–42), He was confronted by men with torches and swords—Roman soldiers and temple guards sent by the Jewish officials, the Sanhedrin—who came to arrest Him (John 18:1–3).

They need not have come in force; Jesus had no intention of fighting. The will of His Father was for Him to pass through the hands of cruel men and be nailed to the tree.

Stepping forward, Jesus asked, "Whom do you seek?" (18:4). "Jesus the Nazarene," they answered (18:5). At Jesus's words those who came to arrest Him fell back (18:6). Jesus asked a second time whom they had come for—they had come for Him (18:7–8).

 DIGGING DEEPER
When Mortal Flesh Meets Majesty
John opened his gospel proclaiming the deity of Jesus (John 1:1–5) and then told us about His humanity (1:14). It shouldn't be surprising, then, that toward the end of his gospel, John gave us a glimpse of deity clothed in human flesh when Roman and Jewish officials came into the garden that night.

John recorded that when Jesus said "I am" to those who came to arrest Him, "they drew back and fell to the ground" (18:6). Some commentators interpret the unexpected collapsing of these battle-hardened soldiers, falling like dominoes, one on top of another, as a surprised reaction to Jesus's sudden approach—as if the solders in the front backed into those standing behind, causing them to stumble and fall.[3] A more likely interpretation is that when mortal flesh met Jesus's majesty, the soldiers' reaction was in keeping with others who have encountered deity (see Ezekiel 1:28; Luke 5:8–9; Acts 9:3–4; Revelation 1:17). And though Jesus's "I am" sometimes referred simply to an acknowledgement of His identification (John 9:9), in light of the solders' response, Jesus's words were probably a revelation of His deity (Exodus 3:14; John 8:58).

Jesus was in complete control; Peter was out of control. At Jesus's command the disciples were allowed to go free (John 18:8–9). But Peter, drawing his sword, lunged and cut off the ear of Malchus, the high priest's servant (18:10). Peter had been with Jesus for three years, yet he didn't understand the high cost of discipleship—the surrender of his will to God's. Jesus rebuked Peter and asked him a penetrating question: "The cup which the Father has given Me, shall I not drink it?" (18:11). In other words, Jesus asked, "Peter, shall I not do what God has willed for Me to accomplish?"

Read Matthew 16:13–17. What was the confession Peter made, and who revealed it to him?

_____

_____

_____

What did Peter do in Matthew 16:21–22? What does this tell you about Peter?

_____

_____

_____

What was Jesus's assessment of Peter's actions? What can we learn from this about Jesus's attitude toward His suffering?

_____

_____

_____

STARTING YOUR JOURNEY

God wasn't through with Peter; Peter went on to pen two books of the Bible and to help establish the early church. More crushing was necessary—because making a disciple is a long and difficult process. Remember, "the conversion of a soul is the miracle of a moment, but the making of a [disciple] is the task of a lifetime" (see chart on page 69). What was true of Peter is also true of us and all disciples of Christ. To those who wish to keep their swords in their sheaths, to deny themselves and drink whatever cup God has for them, here are four realities we must never forget.

First, *for every disciple, there is a purpose to fulfill.* For every committed disciple, God has a divine plan, a God-ordained mandate, a heaven-sent assignment (see 2 Timothy 1:9).

What does Acts 13:36 say about David? And what are the implications for your life?

_____

_____

_____

What is your purpose in life? What is your calling? If you don't know, determine to keep asking God until He reveals it to you.

_____

_____

_____

Are you actively pursuing that calling? Why, or why not?

_____

_____

_____

Second, *with every purpose, there is a cup to drink.* Jesus surrendered His will to the Father and drank the cup of death to fulfill the Father's purpose—the salvation of souls. Fulfilling your purpose as a disciple will entail obstacles and hindrances, but do not let that prevent you drinking deeply from the chalice God gives you.

What setbacks have you faced in fulfilling or finding your calling?

_____

_____

_____

How have you been tempted to quit, to throw in the towel? Explain.

_____

_____

_____

Third, *in every cup, there is a pain to accept and endure.* Obstacles sometimes turn into arduous climbs up seemingly unscalable mountains. We must learn to submit and accept.

What deep disappointments have you known as a disciple of Christ?

_____

_____

_____

How might someone stay committed to Christ during the difficult and dark days of disappointment? What would you tell another who thinks the cost of discipleship is too expensive?

_____

_____

_____

Fourth, *through every pain, there's victory to claim.* "If you share His ghastly if ghostly pain, you'll share His glorious gain," was how Thomas à Kempis put it.[4]

What victories have you experienced as a disciple of Christ? What rewards await you in heaven?

_____

_____

_____

Have you felt the crushing of God's hand? If so, rejoice. He is in the process of turning you from a complacent Christian into a committed disciple. As Rick Warren said so well, "When God wants to make a mushroom, he does it overnight, but when he wants to make a giant oak, he takes a hundred years. Great souls are grown through struggles and storms and seasons of suffering."[5] And who would want to be a mere mushroom when he or she could be a mighty oak?

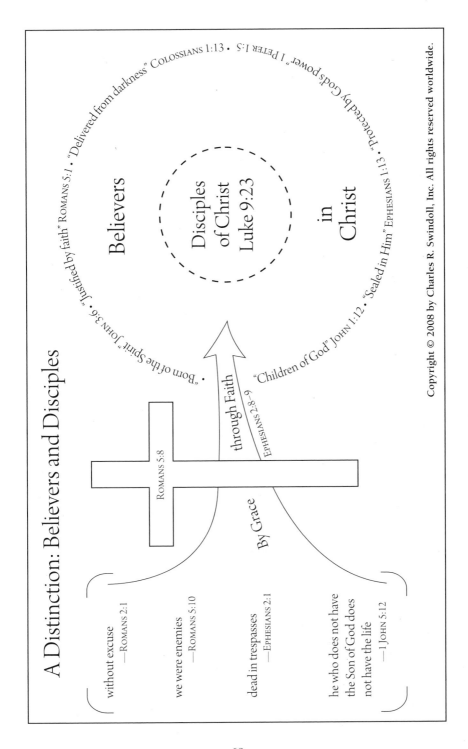

A Distinction: Believers and Disciples

Believers

Disciples
of Christ
Luke 9:23

in
Christ

"Justified by faith" ROMANS 5:1 • "Delivered from darkness" COLOSSIANS 1:13 • "Protected by God's power" 1 PETER 1:5

"Born of the Spirit" JOHN 3:6 • "Sealed in Him" EPHESIANS 1:13

"Children of God" JOHN 1:12

ROMANS 5:8

through Faith

By Grace

EPHESIANS 2:8–9

without excuse
—ROMANS 2:1

we were enemies
—ROMANS 5:10

dead in trespasses
—EPHESIANS 2:1

he who does not have
the Son of God does
not have the life
—1 JOHN 5:12

Lesson Seven

The Lamb That Was Slaughtered
Isaiah 53:3–7

THE HEART OF THE MATTER

These days, we rarely hear someone described as a "person of character." The idea speaks of maturity and integrity and self-sacrifice—a balanced individual who exhibits gentler, as well as consistent, qualities. Yes, the phrase has fallen on hard times. Today our society celebrates the rogue, the rough-and-ready, and the rugged individualist. The meek and mild possess a character too wimpy for the times—or so we think. We are in love with lions not lambs, even though God never calls us lions but calls us lambs (see John 21:15). Because God calls us lambs, perhaps we should think anew about our own character, to see if it is lamblike as was the character of the Lamb of God.

DISCOVERING THE WAY

On April 4, 1968, Martin Luther King Jr. was assassinated in Memphis, Tennessee. That evening, Robert F. Kennedy, hoping to win his party's nomination for the presidency, was campaigning in Indianapolis, Indiana. When news came of King's death, Kennedy's staff tried to dissuade him from speaking to the predominately African American crowd who hadn't yet heard the news. Kennedy refused their advice. Mounting a trailer, he told the audience of King's death and concluded with these moving words: "Let us dedicate ourselves to what the Greeks wrote so many years ago: to tame the savageness of man and make gentle the life of this world."[1]

For Christians, making gentle the life of this world is no meager task when the world doesn't put much stock in gentler qualities such as compassion and love. We live in, as C. S. Lewis put it, "Enemy-occupied territory—that is what this world is."[2]

Do a little brainstorming. In one column write as many words as you can think of that represent lambs. In the other column jot down words that don't represent lambs.

Lambs are . . .	Lambs are not . . .

In general, do you tend to esteem aggressive character traits more than meeker, lamblike ones? Explain why you think that is true or why it isn't true.

_____

_____

_____

_____

Lambs throughout the Scriptures

Lambs are the most significant animals in all of the Scriptures, appearing throughout the Old Testament and the New Testament. Let's trace some of these occurrences . . . and discover their significance.

 Read Genesis 22:1–8.

Abraham was an old man, well past 100 years old, when God came to him with a test (see Genesis 21:5). God directed Abraham to take his son, Isaac, whom he loved more than life—the son through whom God promised He'd build a great nation (Genesis 12:2)—and sacrifice Isaac on an altar. Without questioning, without wrestling, Abraham "rose early" the next morning and obediently did as the Lord commanded. Traveling to Moriah, as God instructed, Abraham and Isaac, loaded with the instruments of worship, began their trek up the mountain. When Isaac wondered, "Where is the lamb for the burnt offering?" his father's reply reflected the great faith Abraham developed over long years of walking with God: "God will provide for Himself the lamb" (22:7–8).

Read Genesis 22:9–13. Tell the rest of the story in your own words.

_____

_____

_____

_____

_____

What does this biblical account tell you about Abraham's and Isaac's character?

Abraham's:

_____

_____

Isaac's:

_____

_____

 Read Exodus 12:3–13.

On the cusp of the Israelites' emancipation after four hundred years of enslavement in Egypt, the Lord commanded Moses and Aaron to instruct the people to take a year-old, unblemished lamb, keep it in their houses for four days, and on the fourteenth day of the month, just before sunset, kill it. The people should then paint their doorposts and lintels with the lamb's blood and roast the meat of the lamb for that evening's meal. During the night, the Lord passed through the land of Egypt and executed judgment on all the firstborn that did not reside under the blood of the lamb.

What significant role did lambs play in Exodus 29:38–39, 42 and Leviticus 23:9–12?

 Read 1 Corinthians 5:6–7.

Corinth, during its day, was a modern metropolis—bustling, exciting, wealthy, cultured, and morally profligate. The church at Corinth had succumbed to the city's wicked ways; it had failed to inoculate the culture with godliness and instead had become infected with the culture's gross ungodliness. Using a metaphor of a rising agent in bread, leaven, Paul sternly reminded them that they were to live lives free of sin, without "leaven." Their boasting of God's grace had cheapened it into license, because just a hint of unrepentant and unjudged sin would spread throughout the congregation, like yeast making bread rise (1 Corinthians 5:6). Paul commanded them to ransack their pantries and throw out the leaven—they should confess their sins and live as though they had been made righteous, which indeed they had. They should never forget that their righteousness had been bought in blood, the blood of Christ, the Passover lamb (5:7).

As we have seen in Exodus 12, what traditional element was consumed along with the unleavened bread at the Passover Feast?

_____

_____

_____

_____

In the biblical passages we've looked at thus far, what was the primary purpose or role of the lamb?

_____

_____

_____

_____

Why do you think Paul called Jesus "our Passover"?

_____

_____

_____

_____

God's Lamb on Earth

Approximately seven hundred years before Jesus's birth, the prophet Isaiah predicted that One would come with lamblike qualities to rescue the souls of men and women. He has forever been known as the Lamb of God.

 Read Isaiah 53:3–7.

God's Lamb, unlike cute and cuddly little creatures, would, according to Isaiah, come into the world and be dismissed and despised. People would reject Him, casting Him off as having no significance in their lives. His "sorrows and . . . grief" would be seen as an embarrassment by power brokers and even the poor, for what could a Man such as He do for them? (Isaiah 53:3). In short, "To a world blinded by selfishness and power, he [would] not even merit a second thought."[3]

As Isaiah predicted, God's Lamb, Jesus Christ, came to earth and was despised because people thought Him weak, when in fact humans are weak. The Lamb only appeared so because He "bore" our griefs and "carried" our sorrows (53:4). Yet making such a sacrifice, to bear away the sins of humanity, only brought Him the esteem given a leper in those days. The world wrongly believed that God punished the Lamb for His own sins, not realizing that it was the rebellion and twistedness of all humanity that led God to condemn the Lamb to a violent and excruciating death, to pulverize Him. As commentator John Oswalt so eloquently wrote: Sin is "the stuff of death and corruption, and unless someone can be found to stand in our place, [sin] will see us impaled on the swords of our own making and broken on the racks of our own design. But someone has been found."[4]

Because the Lamb suffered for humanity—receiving upon His back the lashes that we justly deserved—we find healing for our souls (53:5). But, like sheep, "all of us" have followed our own paths, grazing from one clump of grass to another without concern for our spiritual well-being until we found ourselves lost in our sin. However, the Lord caused the consequences of our "go[ing] astray" to fall upon His Lamb (53:6).

When God's Lamb was roughly treated at the hands of godless men, He did not fight back. Rather, as Isaiah declared, He submitted to being "oppressed," speaking not a word against His inevitable fate—"slaughter" and "shear[ing]" (53:7). God's Lamb was not a victim caught in the cruel killing machine of humanity but the victor who submissively bared His throat to the knife, knowing that His death would save many.

What metaphor did John the Baptist use for the One coming after him (John 1:36)?

_____

_____

_____

How does John's opinion of the Lamb of God in John 1:27–30 compare or contrast with what is written in Isaiah 53:3–7?

_____

_____

_____

Isaiah predicted, John the Baptist introduced, and Peter the apostle affirmed the Lamb of God. Read 1 Peter 1:18–19 and fill in the chart.

Things That Cannot Redeem Sinners	One Thing That Can Redeem Sinners

STARTING YOUR JOURNEY

Lambs are unimpressive little creatures. They don't roar, only bleat and baa. And though cuddly and cute, they don't garner much serious attention. We live in a world filled with lionlike personalities, roaring "Look at me!" But God does not desire proud, self-focused character for His children, His little lambs. He calls us to lamblike qualities, the same ones the Lamb of God exhibited. So, disregarding our lion-obsessed world, let's follow God's own Lamb and adopt these four gentler characteristics.

The first quality: *a life of dependence.* Lambs left all alone are easy prey for prowling lions, but wise lambs recognize their dependence; they stay close to and find protection in the Shepherd.

Have you recently encountered a situation in which you felt like a lamb led to slaughter? If so, explain.

_____

_____

_____

What have you done or are you doing to remedy this problem?

_____

_____

_____

What does Jesus's example in 1 Peter 2:23 suggest you do? How can you apply that to the situation described above?

_____

_____

_____

The second quality: *the assurance of approachability.* No one fears a lamb; everyone fears a lion. Lambs are inviting; lions are intimidating. The world has enough lions; be a lamb.

What positions of authority do you occupy (for example: a boss, a manager, a teacher, a parent)?

_____

_____

_____

On a scale of one to five, how approachable are you? After you've answered, ask someone you trust to rank your approachability.

A Lion		A Roaring Lamb		A Lamb
1	2	3	4	5

How approachable was the Son of God in comparison to His disciples in Mark 10:13–14?

_____

_____

_____

The third quality: *a heart of innocence.* Take a good long look at a lamb and you'll think of innocence. Isn't that what we mean when we call children little lambs?

Look up *innocence* in a dictionary, and write down the definition in your own words.

_____

_____

_____

How is your definition similar to or different from what's found in Romans 16:19?

_____

_____

_____

Is innocence of evil true of your life right now? Why, or why not? And if not, what do you need to do to change that?

_____

_____

_____

_____

The fourth quality: *a spirit of sacrifice.* In Old Testament Israel, lambs existed for sacrifice. The Lamb of God came into the world to sacrifice Himself for the forgiveness of your sins. God calls His children to a life of sacrifice.

What do you think Paul meant in Romans 12:1?

_____

_____

_____

What pleasing sacrifices are listed in Hebrews 13:16? What can you do this week to make this sacrifice to God?

_____

_____

_____

_____

Robert Kennedy spoke of a hope that the savageness of humanity might be tamed, to "make gentle the life of this world." This will not truly come to pass until the Lamb of God returns to earth and establishes His kingdom of justice and peace — when lions and lambs will lie down together (Isaiah 11:1–9). But until that glorious day comes, we must continue to live lamblike lives in honor of our Savior, even in a world of lions. Only then, when our character matches the character of God's own Lamb, will other people be able to look at us and see Him: the Lamb of God.

Lesson Eight

The Cross We Proclaim
1 Corinthians 1:18–2:5

 THE HEART OF THE MATTER
In a society bent on the mad pursuit of appearing self-sufficient, deniers of and believers in Christ alike have slipped into the void of humanism and intellectual pride. We earn advanced degrees while turning our noses up at common sense; we flaunt wealth and possessions while forgetting that moth and rust destroy them; we worship self while convincing ourselves that God will not demand a heavy reckoning.

The apostle Paul warned us to turn our attention away from such worldly foolishness and turn toward the "foolishness" of God—the cross of Christ (1 Corinthians 1:18). The world may think the cross moronic and meek, but only through such divine folly will we become truly wise.

 DISCOVERING THE WAY
An ancient proverb offers wise counsel for those who have ears to hear: "No matter how far you have gone on a wrong road, turn back." How utterly foolish it is to knowingly travel in the wrong direction. Anyone should be able to recognize the truth of this, yet many Christians are enticed to turn toward the dead-end road of humanism, the junkyard that says we find salvation in self-sufficiency. It is only in the cross that we discover the wisdom and power that leads to life.

If you were to write the script for salvation, what would you write?

_____

_____

_____

_____

How would 1 Corinthians 15:1–4 fit into your script for salvation?

_____

_____

_____

Understand the Significance of the Cross

Focusing on Christ's cross will keep us from petty squabbles but, truth be told, a crucified Savior remains a preposterous idea even in today's world. Only God possesses the wisdom to think up such foolishness. However, as Paul argued, the folly of the cross proved wiser than the folly of human wisdom as the means to restore a right relationship with God.

 Read 1 Corinthians 1:18–25.

Paul went to Corinth to preach the death and resurrection of Jesus Christ—but not to preach with a clever tongue that might draw attention to his eloquent rhetoric and diminish the message of the cross (1 Corinthians 1:17). The message, not the messenger, was the important thing. And the message was "foolishness" (in Greek, _moria_—moronic) to the worldly wise, those who walk the silky-smooth pathway of hell. However, the cross "is the power of God" for salvation to those who live according to God's folly (1:18).

Why is this so? The answer lies in Paul's use of Isaiah 29:14, "I will destroy the wisdom of the wise, / And the cleverness of the clever I will set aside" (1 Corinthians 1:19). Since the beginning of humanity, men and women have tried to outwit God or at least to demand that He act according to what they see as wise. But the cross, from the world's perspective, is not wise at all. Yet, what God did through the cross actually revealed the absolute folly of human wisdom to save ourselves.

How does the world today view the message of the cross? Can you cite some quotations or examples?

_____

_____

_____

_____

Have you or someone you know been tempted to outwit God? Explain that situation.

_____

_____

_____

Read Isaiah 40:12–14, 25. How would you answer God's questions?

_____

_____

_____

Paul said that he did not preach the cross with eloquence (1 Corinthians 1:17), but in his defense of the cross against human wisdom, he turned to the rhetorical device of interrogatory—the asking of questions. Paul opened with a general question, calling forth the "wise man," asking where he was (1 Corinthians 1:20). Then Paul specified, asking where were the legal expert, the Jewish "scribe," and the philosopher, the Greek "debater." These "wise men" with their degrees and accolades loved to impress with intricate and nuanced arguments. But the jig was up then, as well as today. Christian philosopher Peter Kreeft called their hand when he wrote, "Most of philosophy . . . has gotten hung up on . . . 'second-order questions,' questions about questions, questions about how to prove things instead of questions about real things."[1]

Paul was concerned about "real things," such as God making "foolish the wisdom of the world" by means of the cross (1:20). Even the Corinthians agreed that worldly wisdom didn't lead to God's wisdom, an understanding of what God did in the world through the cross. Therefore, the ungodly "did not come to know God" because such knowledge only comes through God's power (1:21). This is why it pleased God to commission Paul to preach a message of foolish-ness—because the cross was the "power of God . . . to save those who [put their full trust in Christ]" (1:18, 21).

To prove that human wisdom is really folly and God's folly is really wisdom, Paul reminded the Corinthians that God chose the cross. What have "those who are perishing" chosen (1:18)? With their long history of God showing His power to rescue them, the Jews in Paul's day sought "signs." Greeks, who "were all occupied in the pursuit of every kind of knowledge,"[2] sought *philosophia*—the love of wisdom for its own sake (1:22). But God, instead of giving them the power and wisdom they demanded, gave them a message of weakness and foolishness, the preaching of "Christ crucified" (1:23). The phrase itself, "Christ crucified," is an oxymoron. Christ, the Greek term for *Messiah*, represents power, glory, and victory; *crucifixion* represents weakness, humiliation, and defeat. You can have a Messiah or you can have a crucifixion, but you cannot have both—at least not according to human wisdom. No wonder the Jews saw the crucifixion of the claimed Christ as a *skandalon*, a repulsive "stumbling block" to faith (1:23), and Greeks saw the cross as "madness."[3]

According to Deuteronomy 21:23, why would many Jews see the cross as a scandal?

_____

_____

_____

In contrast, the foolishness of Christ was the power and wisdom of God to save "those who are the called" (1 Corinthians 1:24). Paul concluded his argument against the foolishness of humanity with an axiom: to those perishing, the cross is folly; and so it is God's folly. But the foolishness of the cross proved "wiser [and] . . . stronger than men" (1:25). By the cross, God outwitted the wisdom of the world and revealed their wisdom as moronic; He overpowered His enemies with grace and forgiveness and reduced their strength to an Achilles' heel. Few have said it better than Blaise Pascal:

> Philosophers:
> They surprise the ordinary run of men.
> Christians: they surprise the philosophers.[4]

Consider the Truth of Your Calling

To press the contradiction between the folly of human wisdom and power to save through purely human means and the "weakness" of God's wisdom and power to save through the foolishness of the cross, Paul used the example of the Corinthians themselves.

 Read 1 Corinthians 1:26–31.

Paul reminded the Corinthian church that at the time God called them to salvation, most were the antithesis of the wise and powerful. Paul invited them to think back and carefully consider: according to human standards, few were wise, few were influential, and few were highbrow. In other words, most of them were nobodies by the world's estimation (1 Corinthians 1:26).

Nevertheless, to God, these nobodies were "somebodies"! In choosing these "foolish . . . weak . . . base . . . [and] despised" Corinthians, God chose the "things that are not" to prove that His grace, through the foolishness of the cross, is greater than the world's wisdom and strength; He shamed the world and nullified the "things that are" (1 Corinthians 1:27–28). Therefore, because of God's folly in Christ's crucifixion, the Corinthians had become wise as to "redemption" as well as to "righteousness and sanctification," so that no one could "boast" in his or her self-sufficiency before God. They could boast only "in the LORD" (1:29–31).

What are some common "boasts" used by worldly people to justify themselves before God?

_____

_____

_____

According to 1 Corinthians 1:18–31, what does God say about such boasting?

_____

_____

_____

Hearing the Honesty in Paul's Confession

If the *means* (the cross) and the *people* (the Corinthians) proved that God's folly was wiser than the world's wisdom, then the *preacher* (Paul's manner) would also testify to God's wisdom.

 Read 1 Corinthians 2:1–5.

When Paul walked into the Roman city of Corinth, he did not attempt to distinguish himself through oratorical eloquence or with novel philosophical insights. Paul went to Corinth to "proclaim,"

in simple and plain language, God's good news of salvation—the crucifixion (and by implication, the resurrection) of Jesus Christ (1 Corinthians 2:1–2). Paul was not a rhetorician or a philosopher—two professions highly prized by ancient Romans; he was an apostle commissioned to preach about Christ.

Paul's form of preaching was direct—"Jesus Christ, and Him crucified" (2:2), and his demeanor while with the Corinthians was "in weakness," "fear," and "trembling" (2:3). Paul's weak manner mirrored the message: the "weakness of God" in the cross (1:25). The Corinthians had grown to despise this about Paul because neither his "message" nor his style of "preaching" was to their liking. Paul's style wasn't in the persuasive eloquence of the classic rhetorician. Trembling, Paul relied on the power of the Spirit to demonstrate that the weak and foolish message of the cross was the only means of producing salvation (2:4). The goal of God's folly in the cross, in choosing the Corinthians, and in Paul's weakness was to make the wise foolish and the powerful impotent so that faith rested on the "power of God" alone (2:5).

STARTING YOUR JOURNEY

The foolishness of God is wiser than the wisdom of the world; the weakness of God is stronger than the strength of the world. This was true in the first century when Paul wrote to the Corinthians, and it is true today. And equally true is the temptation to slide into self-sufficiency and an incorrect notion that we no longer need the message of the cross. To ward off that temptation, remember these three wise and powerful principles.

First, *remember the pit*. God is not impressed with a prestigious zip code. He is underwhelmed with wealth, power, and position, but He rejoices over those who never forget the pit of depravity from which they came.

What does Isaiah 51:1 command?

_____

_____

From what pit have you been dug and made righteous?

_____

_____

_____

Second, _refuse the praise._ Arrogance has no place in the life of a Christian. In fact, "The greatest curse in spiritual life is conceit."[5]

Before you became a Christian or recommitted your life to Christ, in what did you "boast"?

_____

_____

_____

Are you tempted to boast in those things now that you follow Christ? Explain.

_____

_____

_____

Paul provided an example of boasting in 2 Corinthians 12:5–10. What was it?

_____

_____

_____

Third, *rely on the power of the Spirit*. Human wisdom and power deceives and will lead you down the dead-end road of humanism and away from the liberty of Christ.

Thinking about an average day, on a scale of one to five how often do you rely on the Holy Spirit to assist you?

Almost Never		Sometimes		Almost Always
1	2	3	4	5

Do you believe that your days could be better if you relied on the power of the Spirit more? Explain.

_____

_____

_____

What does Jesus teach in John 15:4–5?

_____

_____

_____

⟡

If, at a sophisticated cocktail party, you were to confess that you were in love with the Eiffel Tower or describe how you bamboozled billions of dollars from taxpayers or announce that you've decided to become a terrorist, you would gather quite an intrigued and inviting crowd around you. But if you were to confess that Jesus Christ is God, who died and rose again for the salvation of humanity, you'd find yourself in an empty corner with a distinct chill in the air.

The world is not interested in Christ's cross; it is simply too scandalous! Yet we, the saved, proclaim God's weakness and folly as the only wisdom and power to save those who are perishing.

Lesson Nine

Getting Reacquainted with the Spirit of Power
Selected Scriptures

THE HEART OF THE MATTER

Boo! I'm the Holy Ghost. That's what some people think whenever the subject of the Holy Spirit arises. But is He an actual ghost, a mysterious fog-like substance that floats in the ceilings of cathedrals or hovers over cemetery plots like an ethereal phantom? Or is He something completely different? Who is He, really, and what exactly does He do?

Of the three persons in the Godhead, God the Holy Spirit is the least understood and the most mystifying. To many—Christians included—the Holy Spirit is, to borrow a phrase, "a riddle wrapped in a mystery inside an enigma."[1] However, dispelling the myth and mystery is important for our spiritual development.

DISCOVERING THE WAY

"Watch out for ghosts," a mother advised her son. "There isn't anything to them . . . but *if there is*, they're evil."
Attending church the following Sunday, the boy stood with his parents to recite the Apostles' Creed:

> I believe in God the Father Almighty, creator of heaven
> and earth,
> And in Jesus Christ, His only Son, our Lord,
> Who was conceived by the Holy Ghost . . .

Screech! You could hear the brakes of his mind squealing to a sudden stop. *The Holy Ghost? I thought ghosts weren't real, and if they were, they were evil. How could one be holy?* As he mulled this over and the congregation murmured in the background, he heard his parents say, "I believe in the Holy Ghost." That was too much! *They* may believe in the Holy Ghost, whatever that was, but *he* didn't—no matter how holy it was.

It's not just little boys and girls who slam on mental brakes when it comes to the Holy Ghost. Many adults do too. But if we're going to get serious about our spiritual lives, then we must get serious about the triune God, and that means getting serious about the third person of the Trinity: the Holy Ghost or, as He is more commonly called these days, the Holy Spirit.

As best as you can, answer the following questions:

What do you know about the characteristics of the Holy Spirit?

_____

_____

_____

What does the Holy Spirit do?

_____

_____

_____

Blowing the Dust Off the "Holy Ghost" Who Is He?

The mere mention of the Holy Spirit conjures up all sorts of wild speculations as to who or what the Spirit is. To some, He is nothing more than an impersonal "force." To others, He is the most significant person in the Godhead. Neither is correct.

We've been having some fun talking about the "Holy Ghost," but He isn't a ghost. Ghosts remind us of disembodied and tormented souls—existing somewhere between heaven and earth (a phenomenon that doesn't exist). The third person of the Trinity is Spirit; He's *pneuma*, sometimes translated "breath," or that which gives life.[2] Early versions of the Bible rendered *pneuma* as "ghost," but we should refer to Him as the "Holy Spirit." And the Spirit is not an "it" or "thing"; He is a person, possessing "intellect, sensibility, and will."[3]

Read the following verses and record the personality traits or descriptions of the Holy Spirit.

John 16:7–8	
John 16:13	
Acts 5:3–5	
Romans 8:26	
Romans 8:27	
1 Corinthians 12:4, 8–11	
Ephesians 4:30	
Hebrews 10:29	

What implications for your life can you draw from these verses?

_____

_____

_____

_____

We've discovered that the Holy Spirit is a person, but He is not just any person — He is God. The Spirit possesses all the same attributes as God; He is all-knowing (1 Corinthians 2:11), all-powerful (Genesis 1:1–2), always present everywhere (Psalm 139:7–10), and eternal (Hebrews 9:14). The Spirit is known by His divine names, revealing His relationship with the Father and the Son — "the Spirit of your Father" (Matthew 10:20) and "the Spirit of Jesus Christ" (Philippians 1:19) — and revealing His divine characteristics — "the Spirit of glory" (1 Peter 4:14), "the Spirit of life" (Romans 8:2), "the Spirit of truth" (John 14:17), and "the Spirit of grace" (Hebrews 10:29).

Biblical evidence for the deity of the Holy Spirit overflows, but let's focus on one passage: 1 Corinthians 2:6–12.

 Read 1 Corinthians 2:6–12.

In eternity past, God devised the plan of salvation through faith in the death and resurrection of His Son, Jesus; a plan "predestined before the ages" (1 Corinthians 2:7). The result of God's wise plan, worked out on Christ's cross and in the empty tomb, will bring the "mature" to their final "glory" — conformity into Christlikeness (2:6–7). Paul called this a "mystery" or a "secret" (2:7 NIV) — something formerly hidden from humanity in the mind of God but which has now been revealed historically through Christ and made understandable to the "mature" through the Spirit (see Ephesians 1:9; 3:3–4, 9; 6:19; Colossians 1:26–27; 2:2; 4:3).

God's mysterious wisdom was not understood by those who crucified Jesus nor is it understood by those who reject Him today. Paul said, if they had understood the divine mystery "they would not have crucified the Lord of glory" (1 Corinthians 2:8). Anyone to whom the Spirit has not revealed the mystery of the cross and the empty tomb cannot understand the wisdom of God. It is foolishness to them.

Others may not have been able to peer into God's secret wisdom, but to those who love God, He has "revealed [His mystery] *through the Spirit*" (2:10, emphasis added). This truth illustrates the principle of "like is known only by like." In other words, only God can know the mind of God.[4] Diving deep into the divine mystery, the Holy Spirit explores the nooks and crannies of the Father's mind and reveals the truth of the gospel to "those who love [God]" (2:9). Just as only we can know the deep thoughts or "the spirit" of our own souls, so it is with "the Spirit of God" (2:11).

Paul concluded his argument by pointing out the simple truth that the Corinthians, and all who love God, "have received" the Holy Spirit through faith in Christ and that the Spirit has made known—"freely given"—the secret wisdom of God's plan of salvation to them (2:12). But for those who follow the "spirit of the world," those who pursue the folly of human wisdom, the Holy Spirit has not revealed God's deep wisdom because they do not have the Spirit.

Blowing the Dust Off the "Holy Ghost" What Is His Role?

The fingerprints of the Holy Spirit cover the pages of the Bible. We learn of His role in creation; in recording the Scriptures; in ministering to humanity; in relating to us the truths of the life, death, and renewed life of Christ; and His role in the end times. Let's look at four of the Spirit's roles more closely.

 Read Titus 3:5.

The Holy Spirit regenerates us. Because we couldn't save ourselves, no matter how many holy deeds we performed, God the Father mercifully saved us from divine judgment—the consequence of our sins—by sending His Son to die on our behalf. At the moment we believe with faith, God gives us the Holy Spirit to wash us clean and give us new life. The Spirit completely changes our lives by rebirthing us spiritually.[5]

Other passages of Scripture affirm Paul's teaching in Titus 3:5. Read the following verses and jot down how they refer to a Christian's regeneration.

John 3:3–7

_____

_____

2 Corinthians 5:17

_____

_____

Have you been born again? Have you become a new creation? If the answer is no, or if you are unsure, please read "How to Begin a Relationship with God" on page 133 of this Bible Companion.

 Read 1 Corinthians 12:12–13.

The Holy Spirit baptizes us into the body of Christ. Obviously, this doesn't mean Christ's physical body but the universal, worldwide church. Just as we are regenerated and renewed at the moment of salvation, so we are also baptized into, or joined to, Christ's church— His body. Because of that, we are one with—united with—every believer living or dead from the day of Pentecost (Acts 2) to the present time, regardless of race, gender, age, ecclesiastical affiliation, and geographic location. While we are unified in one body, we, by the "sovereign assignment of God . . . [are] given [a] distinct place in the body of Christ [because] every believer is essential to the harmony and perfection of the whole."[6]

 Read Ephesians 1:13 and 4:30.

The Holy Spirit seals us, permanently securing our salvation. Many Christians are terrorized by the thought that they could lose their salvation, that sins they committed after trusting in Christ's work on the cross are so horrible that God will not continue to forgive. How defeating it is to live under such a dark and erroneous cloud. But Paul offered an encouraging word. At the moment of salvation, every Christian is "sealed in [Christ] with the Holy Spirit of promise" (Ephesians 1:13). In fact, though we can "grieve the Holy Spirit of God" by sinning, we cannot lose our salvation because the seal of the Holy Spirit cannot be broken; it is permanent until the day of Christ's return (4:30).

 DOORWAY TO HISTORY
God's Signet Ring

Seals were important objects in the ancient world of the Bible. Usually engraved, like signet rings, seals were made of semiprecious stones, gold, and onyx.[7] Their significance in the Bible was twofold. First, usually with an image impressed in wax, they physically sealed letters (1 Kings 21:8), legal documents (Nehemiah 9:38; Jeremiah 32:10), scrolls (Isaiah 29:11; Revelation 5:1), or doorways (Matthew 27:66). Second, figuratively, seals, like rings, united lovers (Song of Solomon 8:6), symbolized the deputizing power of God (Haggai 2:23), served as a sign of covenant ratification (Romans 4:11), and became a form of identification (1 Corinthians 9:2) and a declaration of ownership (2 Timothy 2:19; Revelation 9:4).

God's seal of the Holy Spirit—His signet ring, if you will—gives assurance that believers in Christ can never lose their salvation; they are secure and safe under the ownership and authority of God.

Do you now or have you struggled with the thought that you could lose your salvation? If so, how evil does one have to be to cross the line from saved to unsaved?

_____

_____

_____

_____

What do the following passages promise?

John 10:29

_____

_____

2 Corinthians 1:21–22

_____

_____

 Read John 16:13.

The Holy Spirit illumines us with the truth. The Spirit was involved in the revelation of divine truth to the men who wrote the Bible, inspiring or "God-breath[ing]" (2 Timothy 3:16 NIV) the infallible words of Scripture. The Bible, then, is not the product of men's creative minds but the product of God's creative breath. These two works—revelation and inspiration—are now complete and have ceased, but illumination continues. Through our prayerful study and with a teachable heart, the Holy Spirit can inwardly "guide [us] into all the truth . . . disclos[ing] to [us] what is to come" (John 16:13).

STARTING YOUR JOURNEY

Why should we take care to learn the truth about the identity of the Holy Spirit and His role? Paul hinted at an answer in 1 Corinthians 4:8, "You are already filled . . . [and] have already become rich [with the mysteries of God]." In other words, the Corinthians thought they had "arrived" spiritually, thinking, *What more could we learn?* It turned out, they could learn a whole lot more because the Spirit had a whole lot more to teach them (see 1 Corinthians 1:6–13). It is easy for us to slip into the Corinthian mind-set; that's why *we must guard against the notion that we have reached the pinnacle of our Christian maturity.*

How mature would you say you are in your relationship with Christ?

Starting to Grow   Still Growing   Fully Grown

1   2   3   4   5

Read Philippians 3:12–13. Who wrote this?

_____

How did he characterize his spiritual maturity?

_____

_____

How does your ranking compare with Paul's description of himself? What implications can you apply to your own pursuit of spiritual maturity?

_____

_____

_____

_____

101

What are the implications for your spiritual growth given the fact that the Holy Spirit no longer gives divine revelation or inspiration but continues to provide illumination?

_____

_____

_____

_____

_____

Far from being afraid or mystified by the Spirit, we should bow in humble adoration. For as John Walvoord so aptly wrote,

> The Holy Spirit . . . [has] the same essential deity as the Father and the Son and is to be worshipped and adored, loved and obeyed in the same way as God. To regard the Holy Spirit in any other way is to make one guilty of blasphemy and unbelief. We tread therefore on most holy ground in thinking of the Holy Spirit of God and the truth involved is most sacred and precious.[8]

Let us tread humbly, for we've a long way to go and the Spirit has much to teach us.

Lesson Ten

What Does Being "Filled with the Spirit" Mean?
Ephesians 5:15–21

THE HEART OF THE MATTER

The Christian life is like a car. You need at least two important things to drive it: a key and fuel. When an individual comes to faith in Christ, he or she is given the key: salvation. But the car of the Christian life doesn't get very far without fuel — the divine enablement of the Holy Spirit, what the Bible calls being "filled with the Spirit" (Ephesians 5:18). As a key and fuel are to the power and enjoyment of a car, so salvation and the Spirit are to the power and enjoyment of the Christian life. And just as we need to refuel to keep our cars going, so we must keep our spiritual tanks full every day to keep growing in our relationship with the Lord. Once we realize this truth — that we need daily and moment-by-moment fillings of the Spirit — we'll live lives of empowerment and authenticity before a watching world.

DISCOVERING THE WAY

C. S. Lewis understood that the Christian life is like a car and that God's Spirit is like its fuel. In *Mere Christianity*, Lewis wrote,

> God made us: invented us as a man invents an engine. A car is made to run on petrol, and it would not run properly on anything else. Now God designed the human machine to run on Himself. He Himself is the fuel our spirits were designed to burn. . . . There is no other. . . . God cannot give us a happiness and peace apart from Himself, because it is not there. There is no such thing.[1]

Few things are more impressive to a lost and watching world than a Christian who maintains this combustible combination: a joyful attitude—Lewis's "happiness and peace"—and an authentic life. Both are fueled by the Spirit of God.

If you were to "build" an authentic Christian, how would this person live his or her life? What elements would not be present?

_____

_____

_____

_____

How close does your Christian life come to meeting your description? Be specific.

_____

_____

_____

_____

A Quick Review of Where We've Been

We saw in lesson 9 that the Holy Spirit is coequal with God and plays a significant role in regeneration, baptism, sealing, and illumination. Jesus provided a concise summary of the Spirit's character and activities through the pens of the apostle John and the church's first historian, Luke, in his book of Acts.

 Read John 14:16–17 and Acts 1:8.

On the eve of Jesus's arrest, knowing that within a matter of hours He would be crucified, Jesus earnestly pressed upon His disciples what would become His last testament. Jesus made a promise: He would ask the Father to send "another Helper" (John 14:16)—a *parakletos.*

A legal word, *parakletos* refers to an advocate, "one who appears in another's behalf," a "mediator" or "intercessor." [2] The combination of *parakletos* and *allos*, "another," would have been a comfort to the disciples because Jesus's promise was that another of His kind (deity) would come and "be with [them] forever" (John 14:16).

The word *parakletos* is also used in 1 John 2:1. To whom does it refer in this passage?

_____

_____

What theological conclusion can we draw about the identity of the Spirit based on the use of *parakletos* in 1 John 2:1?

_____

_____

_____

With God, a promise made is a promise kept. Jesus told His disciples the Father would indeed send the "Spirit of truth," and He would abide "with [them] and . . . be in [them]" (John 14:17). This refers to the indwelling of the Holy Spirit, where the Spirit immediately takes up permanent residence in the lives of everyone who expresses faith in Christ.

What does Jesus promise the disciples (and all Christians) in Matthew 28:20?

_____

_____

_____

_____

In what way is this promise fulfilled?

_____

_____

_____

At the time Jesus spoke the words of John 14:16–17, the Spirit had not dwelt or abided with men and women permanently. But after Jesus's death, resurrection, and ascension, while the disciples were gathered in a large room on the day of Pentecost, the Holy Spirit filled them, just as Jesus promised (Acts 1:8). He said they would "receive power" from the Spirit; they would receive _dunamis_, a dynamic divine enablement to live authentic Christlike lives. In other words, the indwelling Spirit gives us power to control our tongues, our tempers, and our thoughts.

Read Galatians 5:16–23, and answer the following questions.

What is the promise in verse 16?

_____

_____

_____

_____

From the list of fleshly deeds in verses 19–21, write down the ones you've struggled to overcome.

_____

_____

_____

_____

Write down verses 22–23, the fruit of the Spirit, here or on a 3-inch by 5-inch card, and begin memorizing this list.

_____

_____

_____

_____

_____

A Necessary Reminder of
What We Are . . . and Why

Once we've surrendered control of our lives to Christ through the Spirit, we no longer can lay claim to ourselves. We now belong to Him.

 Read 1 Corinthians 6:18–20.

The first sentence in 1 Corinthians 6:18 and the last phrase in verse 20 serve as bookends to this important section of Scripture. Paul commanded the Corinthian Christians to "flee immorality" and to "glorify God" in their bodies (1 Corinthians 6:18, 20). Why did Paul place these emphases on the body when talking about the Spirit?

As an answer, Paul asked his own questions: "Didn't you realize that your body is a sacred place, the place of the Holy Spirit? Don't you see that you can't live however you please?" (6:19 MSG). As soon as the Spirit indwells you — at the moment of salvation — your body becomes His sanctuary. It is unthinkable that anyone could commit immoral acts inside a church, yet we sin with our bodies unthinkingly. We must stop all immorality because "[we] are not [our] own" (6:19).

Why is this true — that we don't belong to ourselves? Listen to Paul's declaration: "For [we] have been bought with a price" (6:20). If we continue in immorality after the coming of the Holy Spirit's abiding presence in our lives, we debase the grace of God and nullify the death of Christ as far as the message we send to others is concerned. This is not authenticity; this is what the world has seen too much of—hypocrisy. "Therefore," Paul concluded, "glorify God in your body" (1 Corinthians 6:20).

Write down a very brief prayer in the following format, asking the Lord to empower you so that you might bring glory to God through your body today.

Dear Lord,

With my mind _____

_____

With my eyes _____

_____

With my hands _____

_____

With my feet _____

_____

 Read Ephesians 5:15–17.

The Message paraphrases the last phrase of 1 Corinthians 6:20 as, "let people see God in and through your body." Paul expressed a similar idea in Ephesians 5:15: "be careful how you walk," because others are watching. Walking wisely—authentically—requires us to buy up, or "mak[e] the most of," our time because we live during desperate days (Ephesians 5:16). Theodore Roosevelt said it well, "Nine-tenths of wisdom is being wise in time." Overcome by the evil of a fallen world, you may have slipped in your Christian walk in the past and made your Christian life something less than authentic. That time is gone. Seize today and glorify God—walk wisely. For as Roosevelt continued, "Let us not advance our unwisdom in the past as a justification for fresh unwisdom in the present." [3]

The notion of making the most of our time was not original with Paul. What did Moses pray in Psalm 90:12?

_____

_____

_____

Paul admonished the Ephesians to put away foolishness and come to a wise understanding of "what the will of the Lord is" (Ephesians 5:17). And what is that? Read on.

An Essential Understanding of How We're to Live

Living authentically—glorifying God and walking wisely—is easily said but not easily done. God understands. That's why He has given us His Spirit, to provide the divine power to live such a life.

 Read Ephesians 5:18–21.

Ephesians 5:18 is one of the most important verses in the Bible for living the authentic Christian life because the final phrase of the verse tells us how to live such a life.

First, Paul admonished: do not be controlled by something that will make your life inauthentic or foolish (Ephesians 5:18). Paul used wine as an example, but we live in a world saturated by all sorts of addictive substances and activities—alcohol, drugs, food, sex, work, television, video games, and the computer. Don't lose control of your life to these temptations.

Instead, be controlled by the Holy Spirit; "be filled with the Spirit" (5:18). This means we are to be characterized by that which fills us—the Spirit—leading to an authentic Christian life. Four factors are worth noting in this simple five-word sentence—"be filled with the Spirit." First, it is an imperative—a command, not a suggestion. Second, it is plural in the Greek; every Christian everywhere is to be filled. Third, it is in the passive voice; the filling is something done *to* us, not something we do for ourselves. Our responsibility is to submit to the Spirit's control, to let Him fill us. Fourth, it is in the present tense; it's not a once-in-a-lifetime event but an ongoing need in order for us to live authentically.

What should a Spirit-filled life look like? Paul offered four telltale signs—four results. First, it will affect your speaking. Your speech will be gracious, uplifting, praiseworthy, edifying, and biblical (Ephesians 5:19).

How might a Spirit-filled person apply Colossians 3:16? (See also Colossians 4:5–6.)

_____

_____

_____

_____

Second, a Spirit-filled individual will have a melodious heart—passionately praising God (Ephesians 5:19). Fred Smith put it succinctly, "Praise is the steam that rises from a warm heart"; from a heart full of the Holy Spirit.[4] Third, a Spirit-filled person will become thankful, exhibiting a grateful attitude (5:20). Gratitude is an eloquent statement of a Spirit-filled soul. Grumbling is an ineloquent statement of a self-filled soul. Finally, being filled with the Spirit will produce mutual submission, motivated by reverence for Christ and His reputation (5:21).

Submission is not a popular notion today. But what did Paul command in Philippians 2:5–8?

_____

_____

_____

Do you struggle with being submissive to the Spirit? If so, what do you need to do about it?

_____

_____

_____

STARTING YOUR JOURNEY

The authentic Christian life doesn't come automatically. It requires us to release our lives to the control of the Holy Spirit. But as Jesus's disciples discovered, living a Spirit-filled life can transform our churches and turn the world upside down.

God determined long ago that He would do His primary work in the world through ordinary but divinely enabled people—the church—rather than through regularly occurring miracles. Therefore, in order to carry forward God's plan, *the church doesn't need monthly miracles; it needs daily enablement.*

Effective churches have pastoral staffs, volunteers, and congregations that are being filled by the Spirit daily. In a general sense, how well do you think your church fits this description? Explain.

_____

_____

_____

What specifically can you do to help foster daily divine enablement in your church?

_____

_____

_____

What the world knows of Christ they learn from Christians. That's too bad, because for too long the world has learned too little of who He really is. As we walk out the door of our churches, the world is watching . . . and thinking, *We aren't looking for the amazing; we're looking for the authentic.*

Living authentically before others is what the world wants and needs from us. How can we achieve authenticity, according to 1 Peter 3:15?

_____

_____

_____

What would a gentle and reverent answer sound like in this world of bombast?

_____

_____

_____

⁂

Brennan Manning, a self-described fool for Christ, wrote,

> The late Romano Guardini once stated that Francis of Assisi "allowed Jesus Christ to become transparent in his personality." If this is what it means to live as a Christian, why are the personalities of so many pious, proper, and correct Christians so opaque?[5]

It is past time that we allow the Spirit to fill our souls and clean the windows of our lives. This is the only way we'll ever live an authentic Christian life; it is the only way a watching world will see Christ for who He is.

Lesson Eleven

Those Unidentified Inner Promptings
Selected Scriptures

 THE HEART OF THE MATTER
God often gets blamed for things He didn't do. But more times than not, He doesn't get credit for the things He did do, because so much of what God does in our lives is not accomplished with fanfare—blowing trumpets or exploding fireworks—but in subtle, unheralded ways. All of us who follow Christ have sensed God's working, even if we couldn't put our finger on exactly what He was doing. This spiritual sixth sense is from the Holy Spirit who indwells every believer and gives inner promptings to God's activities in our lives. But how can we be sure that these unidentified inner promptings are really from the Spirit and not just from our own intuition?

 DISCOVERING THE WAY
Interpreting the little voice inside your head can be tricky. We talk about this inner voice as intuition or a "gut feeling," but rarely do we attribute it to the Spirit's activity. The Scripture says that the Spirit will guide and teach us (see John 16:13–14; Romans 8:14). Writing about the Spirit's guidance, Philip Yancey and Paul Brand concluded:

> Normally . . . God guides in subtle ways: feeding ideas into [the] mind, speaking through a nagging sensation of dissatisfaction, inspiring [us] to choose better than [we] otherwise would have done, bringing to the surface hidden dangers of temptation.[1]

Yet discriminating between His promptings and our own desires or fears is no mean task. Though we are made in God's image (see Genesis 1:26–27), sharing what might be called "natural attributes" with Him—the ability to think, feel, and perceive—many people have interpreted every random thought or feeling as the "voice" of God, leading them into useless, unhealthy, and unbiblical speculations. So, as we look into this delicate subject, let's pray that the Spirit will guide and teach us the truth.

Describe a time when your little internal voice "spoke" to you.

_____

_____

_____

_____

Did you listen? Why, or why not?

_____

_____

_____

How did things turn out?

_____

_____

_____

Would you describe that little voice as the Spirit's prompting? Explain.

_____

_____

_____

Never Forget: We Are "Fearfully and Wonderfully Made"

All of us know, in the depths of our souls, the eternal truth that God exists and that we were created in His image, an image that according to the Psalmist was mysteriously wrought together.

 Read Psalm 139:1–3, 13–14.

There is not one iota of your life that God is not intimately familiar with — not one secret that He hasn't heard, not one fleeting thought that He hasn't perceived, not one sin that He hasn't noticed. This is the point David made in Psalm 139:1–3. God searches and knows and understands everything about us. God "scrutinizes" our lives like someone watching ants in an ant farm; He sees everything we do.

In fact, God's knowledge of us goes back to the beginning, when we were in our mothers' wombs. There, in the secret chamber of your mother's body, God shaped and molded you, weaving together your body and soul, your "inward parts" (Psalm 139:13). For David, such knowledge was too much:

> I thank you, High God — you're breathtaking!
> Body and soul, I am marvelously made!
> I worship in adoration — what a creation!
> (139:14 MSG)

What a creation, indeed! For God didn't just form your material makeup, He formed the immaterial as well — your spirit, which hears the Holy Spirit's voice. By giving us a body, soul, and spirit, God has equipped us with all the internal equipment we need to connect with Him. The entire system is activated at the moment of our salvation.

Which of God's wonderful works did David reference in Psalm 139:13–14?

What did seeing these works cause David to do, according to verse 14?

_____

_____

Reflecting on your answers above, why can we, like David, perceive the wonder of God's works?

_____

_____

Biblical Examples: Those Inner Promptings — Then and Now

The Spirit of God has been active from eternity. And since the creation of humanity, He has been active in guiding and teaching the people of God, as the following biblical examples illustrate. But before we look at these, a word of caution.

As a general rule, when reading the accounts of events in the Bible, keep in mind that narrative is not necessarily normative. In other words, a particular event or outcome in the life of an individual recorded in the Bible doesn't automatically mean that an event in your life will have a similar outcome. The Spirit actively gave inspiration and spoken revelation during Bible times, leading to the creation of the Bible. New words of revelation have now ceased; therefore, the convictions we attribute to the Spirit must be in harmony with God's Word, for the Spirit of God never leads us away from the Word of God.

With that in mind, we're ready to derive four universal principles from four different examples of how the Holy Spirit prompted two different godly men.

 Read 1 Kings 19:9–12.

A little background. Elijah was a godly prophet who challenged the pagan priests of Baal to a contest. After Elijah proved that Baal had no power and the Lord God was the only God, Elijah had the 450 defeated prophets of Baal killed at the Kishon brook (see 1 Kings 18:19–40). Ahab, the wicked King of Israel, witnessed the whole bloody spectacle and told his wife, the equally wicked Jezebel, who in turn sent a death message to Elijah (19:1–2). Fearing for his life, Elijah ran from Mount Carmel, in the north of Israel, to the southern Judean town of Beersheba. From there he escaped to the countryside and hid himself under a juniper tree, wishing to die (19:3–4). Ministered to by an angel, who gave him bread and water, Elijah fled further south to Horeb, in the Sinai desert (19:5–8).

This fugitive prophet of God—the one who had only some forty days earlier killed 450 pagan prophets—climbed into a cave, as far away from Jezebel as he could get, hoping that her hounds wouldn't find him. But the Hound of Heaven did. "What are you doing here, Elijah?" the Lord asked (19:9). The answer was simple; Elijah was cowering in fear (19:10). Commanding His prophet to stand, God had something to communicate, not by wind or earthquake or fire but in the "sound of a gentle blowing" (19:11–12).

 GETTING TO THE ROOT
God's Still, Small Voice

The King James Version of the Bible translates the Hebrew phrase *qol demamah daqqah* as "a still small voice." The New International Version renders it as "a gentle whisper." Did God speak audibly to Elijah in 1 Kings 19:12 as He did in verses 11 and 13, or was this an unidentified inner prompting?

Depending on the context in which it is used, *qol* can mean "voice," "sound," or "noise." *Demamah* is only used in two other places in the Bible, Job 4:16 and Psalm 107:29, and can be translated as "stillness" or "calm," as well as "silence" and "whisper." *Daqqah* refers to something that has been made small, perhaps "thin" or "fine." [2] Literally, we could translate this

Continued on next page

Continued from previous page

phrase as a "thin, calm [silent] sound," indicating that it was different from the audible voice of God in verses 11 and 13. One commentator interpreted the phrase as "The soft voice of God speaking to the conscience, illuminating the mind and stirring resolve."[3]

We learn from Elijah that *the Holy Spirit gives us hope in extreme loneliness and desperation.*

What does Psalm 46:10 command us to do?

_____

What is the connection between stillness and knowing God? What does quietness do for your soul?

_____

_____

_____

How busy is your life? What would you need to adjust to make time for stillness? Are you willing to do that?

_____

_____

_____

 Read Acts 20:22–24.

The apostle Paul knew the same inner promptings from the Spirit of God that the prophet Elijah did. On the docks of Miletus, bound for Jerusalem, Paul spoke to the Ephesian elders, recalling the year he spent among them, the trials they endured, and the message he delivered (Acts 20:17–21). But now, "bound in spirit," Paul faced an uncertain future in Jerusalem; all he knew was what he perceived from the Holy Spirit: "bonds and afflictions" (Acts 20:22–23). Yet Paul would forge ahead because he didn't consider the value of his life as something to hold dear for himself. His life was for the furtherance of the gospel (20:24).

We learn from Paul that *the Holy Spirit brings calm determination in times of threatening fears.*

 Skim Acts 27.

Paul hadn't spent many days in Jerusalem when the Spirit's testimony of afflictions came true. He was arrested and held in prison for two years before being shipped off to Rome for an appearance before Caesar (see 21:17–26:32).

Sailing with "two hundred and seventy-six persons" (27:37), Paul and his companions encountered contrary winds (27:1–8). Perceiving a warning in his spirit, Paul tried to caution his centurion escort to put the ship into port or the "cargo and the ship [and their] lives" would all be lost (27:9–10). Not persuaded, the centurion trusted the seaworthiness of the ship's captain, and on they sailed . . . right into the teeth of a violent storm that lasted fourteen days (27:11–27). Visited by an angel, Paul calmly encouraged the passengers that God would mercifully spare the lives of all on board, but the ship and its cargo would be sunk (27:21–24, 28–44).

We learn from this episode in Paul's life that *the Holy Spirit prompts inner peace in times of potential or present danger.*

Describe a time in which you felt threatened or knew you were in danger.

_____

_____

_____

_____

At any time did you have a sense of inner peace or calm determination? Explain.

_____

_____

_____

 Read 2 Corinthians 12:7–10.

Paul had suffered much for Christ (you can read his résumé of misery in 2 Corinthians 11:23–33), but perhaps the greatest trial Paul endured was his "thorn in the flesh," what he called "a messenger of Satan to torment" him (2 Corinthians 12:7). Three times Paul asked the Lord to pull the thorn; three times the Lord said no (12:8). But somewhere in the pain and struggle, between the prayer and the answer, Paul received a truth deep within his spirit — "My grace is sufficient for you, for power is perfected in weakness" (12:9). Through the Spirit's teaching, Paul understood the paradox of pain — weakness with contentment is great power, if weakness is for the sake of Christ (12:10).

We learn from Paul's thorn that _the Holy Spirit gives greater grace in times of great sorrow and grief._

 STARTING YOUR JOURNEY
Even after these examples, we must still conclude that the Holy Spirit's communication with our spirits is a profound mystery. And because it is mysterious, there is always the risk that we might misinterpret our own desires and fears as coming from the Lord. So what can we do to ensure that we are being led by the Holy Spirit and not led astray by our own "gut feelings"? Follow these two practical principles.

When you aren't sure a prompting is from the Spirit — back off. No one ever lost his or her life by backing away from an unknown edge. However, _when you are sure a prompting is from the Spirit — go forward._

Many have regretted their sluggishness when they knew the Lord was urging them onward. But in both cases, make sure you are walking in the Spirit, as we discussed in lesson 10, and always check your inner voice against the Word of God. God's Spirit produces spiritual fruit and cannot contradict God's Word.

Would you consider it a sin if you knew the Scripture said an action was wrong but you did it anyway and blamed it on a prompting from God? Explain.

_____

_____

_____

What does Psalm 119:9, 11 tell us to do if we want to avoid sin? And what did David pray in verse 12?

_____

_____

_____

Have you hidden God's Word in your heart? Why, or why not?

_____

_____

_____

Do you pray that God will teach you when you open the Scripture? According to John 16:13–14, who is our Bible teacher?

_____

_____

_____

What evidence does being filled with the Spirit produce in our lives, according to Galatians 5:22–23?

_____

_____

_____

How can Galatians 5:22–23 help you determine whether or not your inner promptings are from the Holy Spirit?

_____

_____

_____

⚜

Theologian Vigen Guroian wrote, "The breath of God reaches into even the smallest and most remote garden and human heart and infuses life."[4] Made alive by Christ, our spirits can discern the instigations of the Spirit, if we walk in intimacy with Him and we listen with biblical ears. Only then can we "hear" the thin, silent sounds of the Spirit—those unidentified inner promptings that bring unparalleled peace and fulfillment to our lives.

Lesson Twelve

The Spirit's Most Significant Mission
Luke 1:26–38

 THE HEART OF THE MATTER
The apostle Paul's observation that in "the fullness of
the time . . . God sent forth His Son, born of a woman,
born under the Law" (Galatians 4:4) must be one of the
most significant understatements ever written. Why? Because this
straightforward statement belies the confounding mystery that was
the conception and birth of Jesus Christ. For millennia, Christians—
simple believers and learned theologians—have strained their brains
trying to understand how God became man in the womb of a virgin
girl. So profound is this truth, human minds prove too shallow to
fathom it and words too crude to articulate it. And, yet, the truth
stands squarely on the pages of Scripture, unwilling to budge. So,
as we wrestle with this enormous mystery, know that we will never
master it but must accept it, just as did Gabriel, the messenger of this
truth, and Mary, the recipient of it.

 DISCOVERING THE WAY
Noted scholar John F. Walvoord wrestled with some of
the most confounding notions in the Scripture, leaving
a mound of written works that have helped others
understand profound theological truths. But when it came to com-
prehending the Holy Spirit's role in the conception and birth of Jesus,
Walvoord concluded: "There are few supernatural acts of God which
present a more inscrutable mystery than the [conception and] birth
of Christ. All the elements of the miraculous are present, defying the
reason of man and the normal course of nature."[1]

123

It's unreasonable to assume that reason can know the mind of God because there are any number of natural things that are beyond reason. Reason can explain *how* a child is conceived and born but not *why*. If this is true of natural things, how much more of supernatural things? So, if we are to "understand" the Spirit's activity in the conception and birth of Jesus, we must "reason" with something deeper than reason, something greater than the head — we must "reason" with the heart, with faith.

What does Hebrews 11:3 teach? Do you believe this to be true? Can you prove it? Explain.

_____

_____

_____

_____

What does Hebrews 11:6 require of us? Why?

_____

_____

_____

_____

Tracking the Original Events

The nativity of Jesus Christ was more than the miracle of conception and virgin birth. The events actually began in the temple at Jerusalem, not in Nazareth, and not with a teenage girl but with an old man, a priest. Before Mary received news from Gabriel, he first had been sent to speak with Zacharias, announcing John the Baptist's miraculous conception which would occur in the womb of the priest's aging wife, Elizabeth (Luke 1:11–20). The story ended in an animal stable in Bethlehem, with the angelic host praising God for the birth of Jesus (2:1–7). But in between Zacharias's visitation and Jesus's birth, various bits of the story are scattered between Matthew's gospel and Luke's, making it difficult to keep the events in order. We'll look at Gabriel's announcement to Mary in some detail—the announcement of the Spirit's most significant mission—but the chart on page 132 will help us keep the details of Jesus's conception and birth in chronological order.

Examining the Angel's Message

When we read the story of Jesus's conception and birth, the announcement from Gabriel seems so sudden, so out of the blue. But, in truth, God had planned the events that were about to unfold with meticulous detail a long time before. From before the beginning of time, God had determined the destination of the angel Gabriel and had selected just the right girl from the village of Nazareth to give birth to His Son, the God-man, Jesus. And at exactly the right moment, God dispatched Gabriel to announce to Mary the conception of Jesus.

The prophet Isaiah lived approximately seven hundred years before the birth of Christ. What did he prophesy about Jesus in Isaiah 7:14? What was Jesus to be called? Was this prophecy fulfilled (see Matthew 1:20–23)?

_____

_____

_____

_____

The prophet Micah also lived some seven hundred years before the birth of Christ. What did he prophesy about Jesus in Micah 5:2? Was this prophecy fulfilled (see Luke 2:4–6)?

_____

_____

_____

_____

What do these two prophesies imply regarding God's plan to send Christ to earth?

_____

_____

_____

_____

 Read Luke 1:26–37.

Six months after telling the aging priest Zacharias that he and his wife, Elizabeth, would be blessed with a son who would become a prophet of God, Gabriel stood in the throne room of God receiving another commission to announce another miraculous conception. Sent to the tiny village of Nazareth, in the region of Galilee (Luke 1:26), Gabriel was to speak with a teenage girl, a virgin, whose name was Mary (1:27).

Mary was "engaged" to be married (rather, she was betrothed) to a carpenter by the name of Joseph, a descendant of King David. New Testament scholar Darrell L. Bock, commenting on this ancient Jewish practice of betrothal, the first of a two-stage marriage process, stated,

> The initial stage of engagement (or betrothal) involves a formal witnessed agreement to marry and a financial exchange of a bride price. . . . At this point, the woman legally belongs to the groom and is referred to as his wife. About a year later, the marriage ceremony takes place when the husband takes the wife home.[2]

But before the actual marriage ceremony, the couple were to remain sexually pure.

When Gabriel appeared to Mary, he extended God's grace to her, calling her *charitoo* or "favored one" (1:28). This word refers to a recipient of high praise, and because Gabriel was God's messenger, the blessing came from God.[3] As Bock notes, *favor* is "an expression of divine working . . . [signifying] God's gracious choice of someone through whom God does something special."[4] Mary clearly had no idea what God was up to; her response to Gabriel's salutation was bewilderment (Luke 1:29). Sensing her confusion and fear, and perhaps knowing that the message he was about to deliver would complicate Mary's and Joseph's lives forever, Gabriel repeated his greeting and then dropped the bombshell, the birth announcement of *the* King: "Mary, you have nothing to fear. God has a surprise for you: You will become pregnant and give birth to a son and call his name Jesus" (1:30–31 MSG).

What is the one-word description used to describe Mary in Luke 1:27, 34?

_____

Because this was true, how would an announcement of pregnancy complicate Mary's and Joseph's lives? Think about the reaction of their parents, extended family, friends, and neighbors.

_____

_____

_____

Before Mary had a chance to respond to Gabriel's greeting or announcement, Gabriel stressed three truths about this baby, Jesus. First, His position would be "great" before the Lord. Second, He would be inextricably linked to divinity as God's Son. Third, He would rule Israel as David did, yet His kingdom would never come to an end (1:32–33).

Only now, out of her bewilderment and not out of doubt, was Mary able to speak, saying literally, "How can this be, since I am a virgin?" (1:34). Mary understood the basics of biology. Humanly speaking, the conception of a baby in a virgin's womb was impossible, but Gabriel assured Mary that nothing was impossible with God (Luke 1:37). In fact, and though she did not ask for a sign, she'd be given one: her supposed barren cousin, Elizabeth, was six months along in her own miraculous pregnancy (1:36).

But how? How would Mary become pregnant? This is where we must "reason" with faith . . . we must confess and believe the virgin birth, knowing it's impossible to understand with reason alone.

Gabriel told Mary that there would be a direct and divine intervention in her womb, altering the laws of nature. With two parallel statements, Gabriel simply stated that the Holy Spirit would "come upon" her and "the power of the Most High [would] overshadow [her]" (1:35). Just as God's glorious presence filled the tabernacle (see Exodus 40:34–35) and overshadowed the disciples at the transfiguration of Jesus (see Luke 9:34), so He would envelop Mary. Gabriel didn't say that the Spirit would impregnate Mary, and we shouldn't take these references as sexual in nature. Rather, they affirm the Holy Spirit's active, creative power. Just as God was able to create Adam from the dust and breathe into him the "breath of life" (Genesis 2:7), and just as He was able to breathe life back into the dead body of Jesus at the resurrection (Luke 24), so the Spirit would "come upon" and "overshadow" Mary and place within her womb the divine-human, Jesus. He would be a holy Child whose significance was to be the Son of God, God's Messiah, the One who would "save His people from their sins" (Matthew 1:21).

This significant mission of the Spirit was summed up well by John Walvoord: "The inscrutable mystery can be stated . . . that Christ was begotten of the Holy Spirit; the life which was joined to humanity was that of the Second Person [Jesus (see Hebrews 2:14)], and the First Person became the Father of the humanity of Christ."[5]

Nothing more can be said; this is all we are told of the Spirit's work in the conception of the God-man. It is a mystery too great for our understanding. But it is not a mystery too great for faith—if we will fall on our knees in acceptance as Mary did.

Understanding the Virgin's Response

Mary was perplexed when Gabriel greeted her with a blessing and bewildered when he announced the conception of Jesus. But with the assurance that nothing was impossible for God, Mary stopped her pondering and submitted to the will of God.

 Read Luke 1:38.

   Mary's response to Gabriel's news is an example of the proper attitude we should adopt when the Spirit announces that God wants to use us. First, she was humble — "Behold, the bondslave of the Lord" (Luke 1:38). Second, she was willing to submit her life to God's will, regardless of the potential embarrassment or complications it might cause — "may it be done to me" (1:38). Third, she trusted in the Word of God, spoken through the angel — "may it be done to me according to your word" (1:38).

 STARTING YOUR JOURNEY
Shortly after Gabriel's announcement to Mary, after he left her (Luke 1:38), the Holy Spirit accomplished His mission by conceiving in her womb the embryo of Jesus (see 1:42–43). The Spirit didn't need Gabriel to fulfill His mission, and He didn't need Mary — He could have chosen another girl. Likewise, the Spirit doesn't need our help in proclaiming the mystery of Christ's birth, but as He did with Mary, He favors us with the privilege.

   Therefore, *the Spirit may be sending you out, like Gabriel, to announce the good news of Jesus's birth, death, and resurrection to people who need to hear the gospel.* The Greek word *angelos*, from whence we get our word "angel," simply means "messenger." God may be calling you to be a messenger for Him to someone in need.

What truth did Paul proclaim in Romans 10:13?

_____

_____

What questions did Paul ask in Romans 10:14–15?

_____

_____

_____

How can you apply Paul's words this week? Whom can you speak with about Christ?

_____

_____

_____

What is God's opinion of those who carry the message of the good news according to Romans 10:15?

_____

_____

The Spirit is prodding some to be Gabriels. For others, _the Spirit is persuading you to receive the good news as Mary did—in simple faith._

Reread Mary's response to Gabriel's message in Luke 1:38. How would you describe her attitude?

_____

_____

_____

Read carefully Romans 10:8–10. What did Paul say one needs to do in order to have salvation?

_____

_____

_____

If you'd like to find out more about the good news of Jesus's death and resurrection and what that means for your life, please read "How to Begin a Relationship with God" on page 133 of this Bible Companion.

The conception of Jesus Christ in the womb of a teenage Jewish girl was the most significant mission of the Spirit, and certainly the most mysteriously profound. Strain as we might to understand, in the end we must give up our striving and our unreasonable affection for reason and simply choose to "understand" by faith, to believe that the Spirit conceived the only One who can save our souls. The Scripture promises that someday we will "know fully, even as [we are] fully known" (1 Corinthians 13:12 NIV). On that day, all things will become reasonable.

Important Events Leading to Jesus's Birth

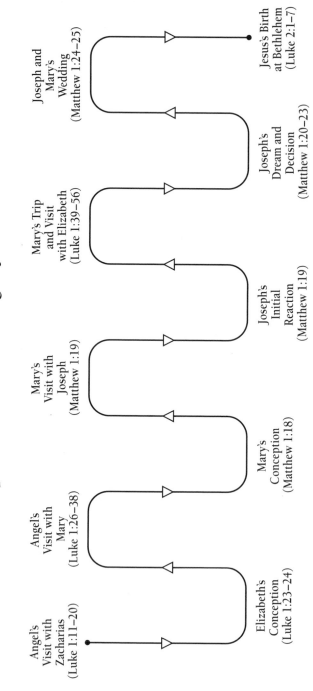

Angel's
Visit with
Zacharias
(Luke 1:11–20)

Elizabeth's
Conception
(Luke 1:23–24)

Angel's
Visit with
Mary
(Luke 1:26–38)

Mary's
Conception
(Matthew 1:18)

Mary's
Visit with
Joseph
(Matthew 1:19)

Joseph's
Initial
Reaction
(Matthew 1:19)

Mary's Trip
and Visit
with Elizabeth
(Luke 1:39–56)

Joseph's
Dream and
Decision
(Matthew 1:20–23)

Joseph and
Mary's
Wedding
(Matthew 1:24–25)

Jesus's Birth
at Bethlehem
(Luke 2:1–7)

How to Begin a Relationship with God

During the days of the prophet Daniel, the wise men of Babylon said of their gods: the gods' "dwelling place is not with mortal flesh" (Daniel 2:11). How true that declaration was, because their gods were not gods at all. How great is our God! There is only one God, the triune God: Father, Son, and Holy Spirit—three distinct persons with the same divine essence—who desire to dwell with humans, or "mortal flesh." In fact, that is the reason God created humanity, to have a loving relationship with us. Unfortunately, our sins—those words, thoughts, and deeds that violate God's holy standard—prevent us from such a relationship. That is why God the Father devised a plan to take care of our sins, God the Son carried out the plan, and God the Spirit makes the plan effective in an individual's life.

Do you have a love relationship with God—Father, Son, and Holy Spirit? Would you like to have such a relationship? If so, the Bible marks the path to God with four essential truths. Let's look at each marker in detail.

Our Spiritual Condition: Totally Depraved

The first truth is rather personal. One look in the mirror of Scripture, and our human condition becomes painfully clear:

> There is none righteous, not even one;
> There is none who understands,
> There is none who seeks for God;
> All have turned aside, together they have become
>   useless;
> There is none who does good,
> There is not even one. (Romans 3:10–12)

We are all sinners through and through—totally depraved. Now, that doesn't mean we've committed every atrocity known to human-kind. We're not as *bad* as we can be, just as *bad off* as we can be. Sin colors all our thoughts, motives, words, and actions.

You still don't believe it? Look around. Everything around us bears the smudge marks of our sinful nature. Despite our best efforts to create a perfect world, crime statistics continue to soar, divorce rates keep climbing, and families keep crumbling.

Something has gone terribly wrong in our society and in ourselves—something deadly. Contrary to how the world would repackage it, "me-first" living doesn't equal rugged individuality and freedom; it equals death. As Paul said in his letter to the Romans, "The wages of sin is death" (Romans 6:23)—our spiritual and physical death that comes from God's righteous judgment of our sin, along with all of the emotional and practical effects of this separation that we experience on a daily basis. This brings us to the second marker: God's character.

God's Character: Infinitely Holy

How can God judge each of us for a sinful state we were born into? Our total depravity is only half the answer. The other half is God's infinite holiness.

The fact that we know things are not as they should be points us to a standard of goodness beyond ourselves. Our sense of injustice in life on this side of eternity implies a perfect standard of justice beyond our reality. That standard and source is God Himself. And God's standard of holiness contrasts starkly with our sinful condition.

Scripture says that "God is Light, and in Him there is no darkness at all" (1 John 1:5). God is absolutely holy—which creates a problem for us. If He is so pure, how can we who are so impure relate to Him?

Perhaps we could try being better people, try to tilt the balance in favor of our good deeds, or seek out methods for self-improvement. Throughout history, people have attempted to live up to God's standard by keeping the Ten Commandments or living by their own code of ethics. Unfortunately, no one can come close to satisfying the demands of God's law. Romans 3:20 says, "By the works of the Law no flesh will be justified in His sight; for through the Law comes the knowledge of sin."

Our Need: A Substitute

So here we are, sinners by nature and sinners by choice, trying to pull ourselves up by our own bootstraps to attain a relationship with our holy Creator. But every time we try, we fall flat on our faces. We can't live a good enough life to make up for our sin, because God's standard isn't "good enough" — it's *perfection*. And we can't make amends for the offense our sin has created without dying for it.

Who can get us out of this mess?

If someone could live perfectly, honoring God's law, and would bear sin's death penalty for us — in our place — then we would be saved from our predicament. But is there such a person? Thankfully, yes!

Meet your substitute — *Jesus Christ*. He is the One who took death's place for you!

> [God] made [Jesus Christ] who knew no sin to be sin on our behalf, so that we might become the righteousness of God in Him. (2 Corinthians 5:21)

God's Provision: A Savior

God rescued us by sending His Son, Jesus, to die on the cross for our sins (1 John 4:9–10). Jesus was fully human and fully divine (John 1:1, 18), a truth that ensures His understanding of our weaknesses, His power to forgive, and His ability to bridge the gap between God and us (Romans 5:6–11). In short, we are "justified as a gift by His grace through the redemption which is in Christ Jesus" (3:24). Two words in this verse bear further explanation: *justified* and *redemption*.

Justification is God's act of mercy, in which He declares righteous the believing sinners while we are still in our sinning state. Justification doesn't mean that God *makes* us righteous, so that we never sin again, rather that He *declares* us righteous—much like a judge pardons a guilty criminal. Because Jesus took our sin upon Himself and suffered our judgment on the cross, God forgives our debt and proclaims us PARDONED.

Redemption is Christ's act of paying the complete price to release us from sin's bondage. God sent His Son to bear His wrath for all of our sins—past, present, and future (Romans 3:24–26; 2 Corinthians 5:21). In humble obedience, Christ willingly endured the shame of the cross for our sake (Mark 10:45; Romans 5:6–8; Philippians 2:8). Christ's death satisfied God's righteous demands. He no longer holds our sins against us, because His own Son paid the penalty for them. We are freed from the slave market of sin, never to be enslaved again!

Placing Your Faith in Christ

These four truths describe how God has provided a way to Himself through Jesus Christ. Because the price has been paid in full by God, we must respond to His free gift of eternal life in total faith and confidence in Him to save us. We must step forward into the relationship with God that He has prepared for us—not by doing good works or by being a good person but by coming to Him just as we are and accepting His justification and redemption by faith.

> For by grace you have been saved through faith;
> and that not of yourselves, it is the gift of God; not
> as a result of works, so that no one may boast.
> (Ephesians 2:8–9)

We accept God's gift of salvation simply by placing our faith in Christ alone for the forgiveness of our sins. Would you like to enter a relationship with your Creator by trusting in Christ as your Savior? If so, here's a simple prayer you can use to express your faith:

> *Dear God,*
>
> *I know that my sin has put a barrier between You and me. Thank You for sending Your Son, Jesus, to die in my place. I trust in Jesus alone to forgive my sins, and I accept His gift of eternal life. I ask Jesus to be my personal Savior and the Lord of my life. Thank You. In Jesus's name, amen.*

If you've prayed this prayer or one like it and you wish to find out more about knowing God and His plan for you in the Bible, contact us at Insight for Living. Our contact information is on the following pages.

We Are Here for You

If you desire to find out more about knowing God and His plan for you in the Bible, contact us. Insight for Living provides staff pastors who are available for free written correspondence or phone consultation. These seminary-trained and seasoned counselors have years of experience and are well-qualified guides for your spiritual journey.

Please feel welcome to contact your regional Pastoral Ministries by using the information below:

United States

Insight for Living
Pastoral Ministries
Post Office Box 269000
Plano, Texas 75026-9000
USA
972-473-5097, Monday through Friday,
8:00 a.m. – 5:00 p.m. Central time
www.insight.org/contactapastor

Canada

Insight for Living Canada
Pastoral Ministries
Post Office Box 2510
Vancouver, BC V6B 3W7
CANADA
1-800-663-7639
info@insightforliving.ca

Australia, New Zealand, and South Pacific

Insight for Living Australia
Pastoral Care
Post Office Box 1011
Bayswater, VIC 3153
AUSTRALIA
1 300 467 444

United Kingdom and Europe

Insight for Living United Kingdom
Pastoral Care
Post Office Box 348
Leatherhead
KT22 2DS
UNITED KINGDOM
0800 915 9364
+44 (0) 1372 370 055
pastoralcare@insightforliving.org.uk

Endnotes

Unless otherwise noted below, all material in this Bible Companion is adapted from the *How Great Is Our God!* sermon series by Charles R. Swindoll and was supplemented by Creative Ministries of Insight for Living.

A Letter from Chuck

1. A. W. Tozer, *The Knowledge of the Holy: The Attributes of God—Their Meaning in the Christian Life* (San Francisco: Harper & Row, 1961), 27.

Lesson One

1. Abigail Adams to John Quincy Adams, quoted in David McCullough, *John Adams* (New York: Simon and Schuster, 2001), 365.

2. Francis Brown, S. R. Driver, and Charles A. Briggs, eds., *The Brown-Driver-Briggs Hebrew and English Lexicon* (Peabody, Mass.: Hendrickson, 2006), 457.

3. John N. Oswalt, "*kabed*," in *Theological Wordbook of the Old Testament*, vol. 1, ed. R. Laird Harris (Chicago: Moody Press, 1980), 427.

4. See Brown, Driver, and Briggs, *The Brown-Driver-Briggs Hebrew and English Lexicon*, 277; and Gerard Van Groningen, "*zaap*," in *Theological Wordbook of the Old Testament*, vol. 1, 247.

Lesson Two

1. A. W. Tozer, *The Knowledge of the Holy: The Attributes of God—Their Meaning in the Christian Life* (San Francisco: Harper & Row, 1961), 2, 27.

2. Tozer, *The Knowledge of the Holy*, 104.

3. John N. Oswalt, *The Book of Isaiah: Chapters 1–39*, The New International Commentary on the Old Testament, ed. R. K. Harrison and Robert L. Hubbard, Jr. (Grand Rapids: Eerdmans, 1986), 179.

4. Tozer, *The Knowledge of the Holy*, 104.

5. Oswalt, *The Book of Isaiah: Chapters 1–39*, 186.

6. Tozer, *The Knowledge of the Holy*, 71–72.

Lesson Three

1. Augustine, *The Confessions*, 3.1.1, trans. Philip Burton (New York: Everyman's Library, 2001), 45.

2. A. W. Tozer, *The Knowledge of the Holy: The Attributes of God — Their Meaning in the Christian Life* (San Francisco: Harper & Row, 1961), 97.

Answer key to the matching exercise on page 27.
1. G, 2. E, 3. J, 4. H, 5. B, 6. I, 7. A, 8. C, 9. F, 10. D.

Lesson Four

1. Mary Wollstonecraft Shelley, *Frankenstein*, (New York: Barnes & Noble Classics, 2003), 196.

2. A. W. Tozer, *The Knowledge of the Holy: The Attributes of God — Their Meaning in the Christian Life* (San Francisco: Harper & Row, 1961), 93.

3. Francis Brown, S. R. Driver, and Charles A. Briggs, eds., *The Brown-Driver-Briggs Hebrew and English Lexicon* (Peabody, Mass.: Hendrickson, 2006), 338.

4. C. S. Lewis, *Surprised by Joy: The Shape of My Early Life* (San Diego, Calif.: Harcourt Brace Jovanovich, 1955), 227.

5. Shelley, *Frankenstein*, 197.

Lesson Five

1. John Bunyan, *The Pilgrim's Progress: From This World to That Which Is to Come* (Westwood, N.J.: Barbour and Co., 1985), 36.

2. Frederick William Danker, ed., *A Greek-English Lexicon of the New Testament and Other Early Christian Literature*, 3d rev. ed. (Chicago: University of Chicago Press, 2000), 989.

3. Kenneth S. Wuest, "Philippians in the Greek New Testament," in *Wuest's Word Studies: From the Greek New Testament*, vol. 2 (Grand Rapids: Eerdmans, 1973), 62.

4. Wuest, "Philippians in the Greek New Testament," 65.

5. Wuest, "Philippians in the Greek New Testament," 67.

6. Donald Guthrie, *New Testament Introduction* (Downers Grove, Ill.: InterVarsity, 1970), 540.

7. Marcus Tullius Cicero, "The Speech of M. T. Cicero in Defence of Ciaus Rabirius, Accused of Treason," sec. 5, in *The Orations of Marcus Tullius Cicero*, vol. 2, trans. C. D. Yonge (London: G. Bell and Sons, 1917), 269.

8. William Wilberforce, *A Practical View of Real Christianity*, ed. Chuck Stetson (McLean, Va.: Trinity Forum, 2007), 39.

Lesson Six

1. Alan Redpath, quoted in Charles R. Swindoll, *Laugh Again: Experience Outrageous Joy* (Dallas: Word, 1991), 146.

2. A. W. Tozer, *The Root of the Righteous* (Camp Hill, Pa.: Christian Publications, 1986), 137.

3. See Leon Morris, *The Gospel According to John,* The New International Commentary on the New Testament (Grand Rapids: Eerdmans, 1984), 743–44. Morris doesn't take this position but offers it as a possibility.

4. Thomas à Kempis, *The Imitation of Christ: How Jesus Wants Us to Live*, trans. William Griffin (San Francisco: HarperSanFrancisco, 2000), 83.

5. Rick Warren, *The Purpose Driven Life: What on Earth Am I Here For?* (Grand Rapids: Zondervan, 2002), 222.

Lesson Seven

1. Robert F. Kennedy, "Statement on the Assassination of Martin Luther King, Jr.," April 4, 1968, http://www.rfkmemorial. org/lifevision/assassinationofmartinlutherkingjr (accessed March 5, 2009).

2. C. S. Lewis, *Mere Christianity* (San Francisco: HarperSanFrancisco, 2001), 46.

3. John N. Oswalt, *The Book of Isaiah: Chapters 40–66,* The New International Commentary on the Old Testament, ed. R. K. Harrison and Robert L. Hubbard, Jr., (Grand Rapids: Eerdmans, 1998), 384.

4. Oswalt, *The Book of Isaiah,* 387.

Lesson Eight

1. Peter Kreeft, *Between Heaven and Hell: A Dialog Somewhere Beyond Death with John F. Kennedy, C. S. Lewis and Aldous Huxley* (Downers Grove, Ill.: InterVarsity, 1982), 37.

2. Herodotus, *The Histories*, 4.77, trans. George Rawlinson (New York: Everyman's Library, 1997), 334.

3. Justin Martyr, *The First Apology*, 13, in *St. Justin Martyr the First and Second Apologies*, trans. Leslie William Barnard, Ancient Christian Writers: The Works of the Fathers in Translation (New York: Paulist, 1997), 31.

4. Blaise Pascal, *Pensées*, 613, trans. A. J. Krailsheimer (New York: Penguin Books, 1995), 206.

5. Oswald Chambers, *My Utmost for His Highest* (Uhrichsville, Ohio: Barbour, n.d.), January 12.

Lesson Nine

1. Winston S. Churchill, "The First Month of the War," October 1, 1939, in *Churchill Speaks, 1897–1963: Collected Speeches in Peace and War*, ed. Robert Rhodes James (New York: Barnes & Noble Books, 1998), 694.

2. Frederick William Danker, ed., *A Greek-English Lexicon of the New Testament and Other Early Christian Literature*, rev. 3d ed. (Chicago: University of Chicago Press, 2000), 832.

3. John F. Walvoord, *The Holy Spirit: A Comprehensive Study of the Person and Work of the Holy Spirit* (Grand Rapids: Academie Books, 1958), 6.

4. See Gordon D. Fee, *The First Epistle to the Corinthians*, The New International Commentary on the New Testament (Grand Rapids: Eerdmans, 1987), 110.

5. For "regeneration" (*paliggenesia*), see Danker, *A Greek-English Lexicon of the New Testament and Other Early Christian Literature*, 752; for "renewal" (*anakainosis*), see Danker, 65.

6. Walvoord, *The Holy Spirit*, 141.

7. See Larry G. Herr, "Seal," in *The International Standard Bible Encyclopedia*, vol. 4, Q–Z (Grand Rapids: Eerdmans, 1988), 369.

8. Walvoord, *The Holy Spirit*, 5.

Lesson Ten

1. C. S. Lewis, *Mere Christianity* (San Francisco: HarperSanFrancisco, 2001), 50.

2. Frederick William Danker, ed., *A Greek-English Lexicon of the New Testament and other Early Christian Literature*, rev. 3d ed. (Chicago: University of Chicago Press, 2000), 766.

3. Theodore Roosevelt to Newton D. Baker, April 22, 1917, in *Theodore Roosevelt Cyclopedia*, ed. Albert Bushnell Hart and Herbert Ronald Ferleger, rev. 2d ed. (Westport, Conn.: Meckler; Oyster Bay, N.Y.: Theodore Roosevelt Association, 1989), 453, http://www.theodoreroosevelt.org/TR%20Web%20Book/TR_CD_to_HTML490.html (accessed March 27, 2009).

4 Fred Smith, *You and Your Network: Getting the Most Out of Life* (Waco, Tex.: Key-Word Books, 1984), 198.

5. Brennan Manning, *The Importance of Being Foolish: How to Think Like Jesus* (San Francisco: HarperSanFrancisco, 2005), 37.

Lesson Eleven

1. Paul Brand and Philip Yancey, *In His Image*, in Paul Brand and Philip Yancey, *In the Likeness of God: The Dr. Paul Brand Tribute Edition of* Fearfully and Wonderfully Made *and* In His Image (Grand Rapids: Zondervan, 2004), 452.

2. See Gene Rice, *Nations Under God: A Commentary on the Book of 1 Kings* (Grand Rapids: Eerdmans, 1990), 160.

3. Donald J. Wiseman, *1 and 2 Kings: An Introduction and Commentary*, Tyndale Old Testament Commentaries (Downers Grove, Ill.; Leicester, England: InterVarsity, 1993), 173.

4. Vigen Guroian, "Inheriting Paradise," in *Books and Culture: A Christian Review*, July 1, 1999, http://www.christianitytoday.com/bc/1999/julaug/9b4015.html (accessed April 1, 2009).

Lesson Twelve

1. John F. Walvoord, *The Holy Spirit: A Comprehensive Study of the Person and Work of the Holy Spirit*, 3d ed. (Grand Rapids: Academie/Zondervan, 1958), 83.

2. Darrell L. Bock, *Luke, Volume 1: 1:1–9:50*, Baker Exegetical Commentary on the New Testament, ed. Moisés Silva (Grand Rapids: Baker Books, 1999), 107.

3. Frederick William Danker, ed., *A Greek-English Lexicon of the New Testament and Other Early Christian Literature*, rev. 3d ed. (Chicago: University of Chicago Press, 2000), 1081.

4. Bock, *Luke, Volume 1: 1:1–9:50*, 111.

5. Walvoord, *The Holy Spirit*, 84.

Resources for Probing Further

God declared,

> "My thoughts are not your thoughts,
> Nor are your ways My ways. . . .
> For as the heavens are higher than the earth,
> So are My ways higher than your ways
> And My thoughts than your thoughts."
> (Isaiah 55:8–9)

Could there be a subject any more difficult to understand than the subject of God—Father, Son, and Holy Spirit? Men and women spend lifetimes trying to reach the highest of God's thoughts, and still they fall short. But this shouldn't deter us from stretching our minds and reaching out because, though much of our God is mysterious and unknowable, much is not—as we've seen in this study of *How Great Is Our God!*

To know our God better, we should diligently examine the Scriptures (see Acts 17:11). But we should also read and study what others have written about our God. So to further your study of our great God, we recommend the following resources. Of course, we cannot always endorse everything a writer or ministry says in these works, so we encourage you to approach these and all other nonbiblical resources with wisdom and discernment.

Carson, D. A. *The Difficult Doctrine of the Love of God.* Wheaton, Ill.: Crossway Books, 2000.

Demarest, Bruce. *The Cross and Salvation: The Doctrine of Salvation.* Wheaton, Ill.: Crossway Books, 2006.

Erickson, Millard J. *The Word Became Flesh: A Contemporary Incarnational Christology.* Grand Rapids: Baker Book House, 1991.

Ingram, Chip. *God: As He Longs for You to See Him*. Grand Rapids: Baker Books, 2004.

Lutzer, Erwin W. *Cries from the Cross: A Journey into the Heart of Jesus*. Chicago: Moody, 2002.

Packer, J. I. *Keep in Step with the Spirit: Finding Fullness in Our Walk with God*. Grand Rapids: Baker, 2005.

Sproul, R. C. *The Holiness of God*, 2d ed. Wheaton, Ill.: Tyndale House. 1998.

Swindoll, Charles R. *Flying Closer to the Flame: A Passion for the Holy Spirit*. Dallas: Word, 1993.

Swindoll, Charles R. *Growing Deep in the Christian Life*. Grand Rapids: Zondervan, 1995.

Swindoll, Charles R. *Jesus: The Greatest Life of All*. Nashville: Thomas Nelson, 2008.

Swindoll, Charles R., and Roy B. Zuck, eds. *Understanding Christian Theology*. Nashville: Thomas Nelson, 2003.

Tozer, A. W. *The Knowledge of the Holy*. New York: HarperCollins, 1992.

Tozer, A. W. *The Pursuit of God*. Camp Hill, Pa.: WingSpread Publishers, 2007.

Ordering Information

If you would like to order additional copies of *How Great Is Our God! Bible Companion* or order other Insight for Living resources, please contact the office that serves you.

United States

Insight for Living
Post Office Box 269000
Plano, Texas 75026-9000
USA
1-800-772-8888
Monday through Friday,
7:00 a.m. –7:00 p.m.
Central time
www.insight.org
www.insightworld.org

Canada

Insight for Living Canada
Post Office Box 2510
Vancouver, BC V6B 3W7
CANADA
1-800-663-7639
www.insightforliving.ca

Australia, New Zealand, and South Pacific

Insight for Living Australia
Post Office Box 1011
Bayswater, VIC 3153
AUSTRALIA
1 300 467 444
www.insight.asn.au

United Kingdom and Europe

Insight for Living United Kingdom
Post Office Box 348
Leatherhead
KT22 2DS
UNITED KINGDOM
0800 915 9364
www.insightforliving.org.uk

Other International Locations

International constituents may contact the U.S. office through our Web site (www.insightworld.org), mail queries, or by calling +1-972-473-5136.